PROSE
APPRECIATION
FOR A-LEVEL

JOHN CADDEN

Edward Arnold

© **1984 Federal Publications (S) Pte Ltd**

First published in Great Britain 1986 by
Edward Arnold (Publishers) Ltd, 41 Bedford Square, London WC1B 3DQ

Edward Arnold (Australia) Pty Ltd, 80 Waverley Road, Caulfield East,
Victoria 3145, Australia

ISBN 0 7131 7610 5

Printed in Singapore by Fu Loong Lithographer Pte Ltd

PREFACE

This book is designed as a companion to the earlier *Poetry Appreciation For A-Level*. Much of what was said in that book is equally relevant to the analysis of prose. This book deals with the elements of analysis that are more specifically related to prose. Yet prose basically involves less in terms of 'technical' background, so the emphasis here will be mainly on practical application. The intention is to provide the Advanced Level student with ample scope for written and oral practice and to offer the student a wide range and variety of prose writing.

The subtleties of prose are different from those of poetry. The prose writer generally takes more of the reader's time, spends more time in his company, if you like, and usually tries to establish a bond or rapport with his reader. Indeed, the prose writer tends to be more aware of his reader and the reader's likely response. (Many poets write poems primarily for themselves, rather than any reader — as a form of self-understanding, release, or 'therapy'.) As with poetry, the manner in which a student *approaches* prose appreciation is of crucial importance. If he approaches a prose passage with fears of being 'tested', or 'caught out', or as a puzzle to be deciphered, or a chore to be completed — then such a 'rapport' is unlikely to be achieved.

All writers have one simple aim — to be understood as fully as possible. The means they might employ to achieve this 'full' communication will not be used merely for the sake of 'cleverness', or obscurity (masquerading as profundity). If a student can see a writer as someone with something to say to *him*, as a person, about something that the writer considers important or interesting, such a student will already be on the way to approaching all literature in the 'true spirit'.

CONTENTS

CHAPTER 1

THE NATURE
OF PROSE

GENERAL CONSIDERATIONS

It is unfortunate that prose is often seen as the opposite of poetry. In a sense, it is inevitable; any formal, written communication has to be either prose or poetry. Yet this contrary association tends to suggest that prose is in some way inferior to poetry — lacking the subtlety, ingenuity, or power of verse. The adjective 'prosaic' has even stronger connotations of something mundane, tedious, or unimaginative. Our daily familiarity with prose — on packets, in newspapers, notices, etc. — perhaps deadens us further to its true potential. There is another difficulty for the student. Poetry tends to 'play' with language more elaborately and obviously. It draws more attention to its use of language and is, consequently, easier to comment on in detail. With prose, language is more unobtrusive, and the reader tends to concentrate more on the flow of plot, character or idea. Poetry can also be offered to the student complete, whereas prose is nearly always, inevitably, looked at in 'extract' form — thus allowing the student only a partial glimpse of the total, integrated whole.

Prose and poetry are not opposites; they are simply different means of communication that offer the writer different possibilities in the treatment of his material. One of the most significant developments of modern literature has been a deliberate obscuring of the traditional boundaries between poetry and prose. Traditionally, poetry followed conventions of form and metrical patterning, yet the prose of a writer such as James Joyce is as meticulous and sustained in its construction as any poem. At the same time, many modern poets have attempted deliberately 'prosaic' effects in their poems, as in Edward Thomas's 'Up in the Wind':

> I could wring the old thing's neck that put it there!

1

A public house! it may be public for birds,
Squirrels, and such-like . . . .

or Roger McGough's 'Poem for a Dead Poet':

He was a poet he was.
A proper poet.
He said things
that made you think
and said them nicely.

To go even further back, three 'epic' poems — the Anglo-Saxon *Beowulf*, Chaucer's *Canterbury Tales* and Milton's *Paradise Lost* — have all had critics claiming them to be the first English novel.

Poetry was traditionally seen as the medium for memorable evocations of descriptive atmosphere, with its elaborate abundance of imagery. Yet few poems can match the rich intensity of detail in the finest passages from a novel by Hardy, or Conrad. The personal, intimate and subjective potential of poetry was considered more appropriate for deeply emotive writing — yet the prose of Emily Bronte or D H Lawrence can be as passionate and as moving as any Romantic poem.

All the arts have been subject to considerable re-evaluation and experimentation in our present century — and prose-writing has also developed. The short story became a firmly established literary genre. Novels, seeking greater 'psychological' accuracy and deeper characterization, evolved concepts of 'interior monologue' and the 'stream of consciousness'. Virginia Woolf, and others, sought to achieve 'prose poems', or genuinely 'poetic' novels. The golden age of 'letter writing' and the 'essayist' may well have passed, yet autobiographies and memoirs have proliferated in modern times. Serious journals, newspapers and magazines have also ensured a continuing flow of quality prose of a contemplative or philosophical nature.

THE FUNCTION OF PROSE

The type of prose-writing varies according to its intended purpose. Yet whether the writer is offering instructions for assembling a hi-fi unit, or a guide book to the chateaus of France, or a history of the tribes of Lower Somalia, or a doctorate on existentialism, or a novel, certain virtues are always at a premium in well-written prose. These are: clarity, precision and a logical, coherent flow and organization of ideas. It is not that such

2

elements are not also present in poetry — but they are more crucially emphasized and necessary in prose.

The basic reason for this is that poetry *suggests*, whereas prose *states*. Prose can work — and work well — in the manner of poetry, through association, suggestion, imagery, etc. yet what it has to say is more specific and clearly defined. We can react differently to a poem, or to different parts of a poem, in terms of its basic meaning, from other readers. Within ourselves, we may react differently to the same poem at different times in our lives. Yet there is much less ambiguity with prose — and if ambiguity can be a positive strength behind great poetry (as in, say, the 'Ode on a Grecian Urn' by Keats), it is generally a weakness in prose.

PROSE AND THE STUDENT

Of the many different types of prose, the student of Advanced Level English will be concerned mainly with the prose of novels, short stories and essays. 'Literary' prose in its widest sense will come from a writer who has thought deeply about what he has to say and the best way of saying it and will reveal a command of language and structure to enhance its effectiveness. (A letter to a bank manager requesting a loan may possess the former, but not necessarily the latter.)

A student attempting to 'appreciate' a prose passage basically works through three questions:

1. What is the writer trying to say?
2. What means does he employ towards effective communication?
3. How successful is he?

PRESENT FORMAT

This book will follow a similar format to the previous book *Appreciating Poetry for A-Level*. Different aspects of prose appreciation and analysis will be discussed in separate chapters. Where appropriate, short exercises will conclude each chapter to highlight what has been discussed. To give our analysis practical application, there will be several 'Reference Passages'. These will be given at the beginning and constantly referred to, so that the different elements of prose analysis may be observed 'in action'.

It is somewhat artificial to isolate prose appreciation into separate elements, so the final section will attempt to pull the various strands together and deal specifically with how the student may confront written analyses and examinations. This will include specimen answers, full length exercises and past questions from Advanced Level examinations.

CHAPTER 2

THE
DEVELOPMENT
OF PROSE

Over the centuries, prose writing has been far less subject to change and innovation than poetry. Its formal arrangement of grammar, sentence and paragraph is less open to experimentation and the developments of prose have been largely stylistic — as opposed to the frequently drastic expansions of form and structure in poetry. It is desirable for A-level students to have some awareness of this stylistic development, as it will provide a context and a framework for the discussion of any given passage. Many students feel any passage that is not overtly modern is going to provide them with impenetrable mysteries of syntax and vocabulary and inwardly create their own barrier towards understanding such 'ancient' texts. Yet the difficulties that will arise here are largely on the surface and will, in themselves, present few problems for the well-read student.

The following is an extremely broad outline of the main characteristics of the different eras of English prose writing. It is only suggested as a general, introductory guide to the main landmarks. The student will obtain most use from this 'survey' by familiarizing himself with the given examples and availing himself as far as possible of the suggested further reading. The texts indicated, by and large, represent the more typical aspects of the age in question and can easily be sampled in random extracts rather than in their entirety if time does not allow for complete readings.

A-Level examiners do not set passages written before 1500, so we may safely begin with these two centuries. This age saw the birth of many of the modern sciences; it was, after all, the age of Galileo and Newton. It also produced the English Civil War (with its central controversy of a divinely appointed monarch and a democratically elected 'commonwealth' government) and saw the rise of Puritanism. Consequently it was a time of the questioning of traditional beliefs and adjusting to new ideas. The prose writing of this period reflects these concerns. The most common form of such writing was the essay, or treatise. Such essays are almost exclusively characterized by themes of religion, 'reason', science and politics. They were intended almost exclusively for instruction or edification, and are nearly always didactic in tone.

Most students will find the 'style' (i.e. language, grammar, spelling, punctuation, sentence and paragraph structuring) of such writing somewhat unfamiliar. The language will appear archaic and outmoded. Spelling and punctuation are personalized and arbitrary. (In fact, they were not finally formulated until the late nineteenth-century). Rules of grammar were heavily influenced by Latin — which produces the characteristically long sentences, laced with intricate clause patterns, which are the most obvious characteristic of such writing.

The Classical models were obsessively revered for their elegance and balance of construction. Yet English is not Latin and this, at times slavish, imitation frequently makes the prose of this period, with its weighty philosophical content, genuinely heavy going. Such passages as the student is likely to come across will have a 'formal' or 'elevated' tone about them and an 'intellectual' or 'learned' manner. In keeping with the 'scientific' age, there is an attempt to make prose as direct and precise as possible. Figurative language, imagery and metaphor are often seen as unnecessary distractions — although two of the finest prose writers of the time, Donne and Milton (both primarily poets), are obvious exceptions. The following example is from Milton's "Establishing a Commonwealth" (full title of original pamphlet "The Readie and Easie Way to Establish a Free Commonwealth", 1660).

> Considering these things so plain, so rational, I cannot but yet further admire on the other side, how any man, who hath the true principles of justice and religion in him, can presume or take upon him to be a king and lord over his brethren, whom he cannot but know, whether as men or Christians, to be for the

most part every way equal or superior to himself: how he can display with such vanity and ostentation his regal splendour, so supereminently above other mortal men; or, being a Christian, can assume such extraordinary honour and worship to himself, while the kingdom of Christ, our common king and lord, is hid to this world, and such gentilish imitation forbid in express words by himself to all his disciples.

In terms of theme and style, the student should already be able to distinguish much that is typical here. The passage centres on an egalitarian dismissal of monarchs and autocrats. There is an opening appeal to 'reason' as the only real basis for serious contemplation. The entire passage constitutes one sentence, yet the sense and clarity are maintained by the controlling force of comma, colon and semi-colon. In the hands of such a skilful writer, the complex sentence does not become rambling or convoluted and will build to a firm and emphatic conclusion — with the full force of all that has gone before adding increased conviction and momentum to the final point.

If the multitude of subordinate clauses, modifiers and parenthetical comments are not coherently and tightly structured such writing will quickly 'lose' its reader. There is also the danger of bathos (i.e. 'anticlimax'), should the final comment not merit such elaborate preparation. The actual archaic nature of the language ("I cannot but yet further admire . . . ." used in its original Latin sense of 'wonder, or be amazed at') should not present any problem that careful reading will not solve. Similarly, the strident, authoritative, confident (some would say over-confident) tone of such writing may be unexpected for a reader who has previously only been acquainted with 'modern' prose (unless this reading has included the essays of D H Lawrence!), yet again this hardly constitutes a serious obstacle to basic understanding.

If the student is prepared to work through the complex structures of sixteenth and seventeenth century prose, unravelling their elaborate, yet logical links, he will enjoy the fruits of some of the keenest minds and committed thinkers of the age.

Suggested Further Reading

Sir Philip Sidney, *The Defence of Poesie* (1597)
Francis Bacon, *Essays* (1620)
John Donne, *Sermons* (1631)
John Milton, *Areopagitica* (1644)
John Bunyan, *The Pilgrim's Progress* (1678)
Samuel Pepys, *Diaries* (1669)

If the age we have just looked at may be termed the 'Age of Science', it was followed by the 'Age of Reason'. Again this is an unsatisfactory generalization, but it does serve to highlight the general temperament of the age. Once more, the writers of the time are deeply in tune with contemporary concerns. People had now learned to trust the new sciences and tended to feel that all aspects of life could be logically and rationally quantified. In the prose of the time we find a concentration on the intellect (as opposed to the emotions) — argument, wit, thesis, satire — and nearly always in praise of realistic moderation and pragmatism. The style of the age was more concerned with precision and eloquence of expression, rather than innovation or experiment ("What oft was thought yet ne'er so well expressed"). Good taste and good sense were what the age expected from its writers.

It is a crucial age for English prose, for it saw the concentrated development of the novel as a fully-fledged literary form. The early novelists, amazingly enough, encompass between them nearly all the 'technical' variations of the novel that were to be more fully developed by later ages. Richardson adopts an epistolary technique (i.e. making the novel a series of 'letters'); Fielding employs the picaresque (i.e. using a series of extravagant adventures, usually connected with a journey); Swift and Defoe explore the possibilities of fantasy; Sterne, in *Tristram Shandy*, the one genuinely innovative piece of prose of its time, makes rudimentary explorations into the possibilities of 'stream of consciousness'. Along with Smollett, this group of writers constitutes the first novelists. Nearly all write with a sense of detachment, finely developing the potential of prose for ironic and satiric statement.

Such prose will still appear unfamiliar to the student initially, although there is an increasing consistency of spelling, grammar and punctuation. Sentence structure, mercifully, also becomes more manageable. The following example is from one of the most luminous literary lights of the age, Dr Johnson. He is talking here of Gray's famous poem, "Elegy in a Country Churchyard":

> In the character of his Elegy I rejoice to concur with the
> common reader; for by the common sense of readers
> uncorrupted with literary prejudices, after all the refinements of
> subtility and the dogmatism of learning, must be finally decided
> all claim to poetical honours. The churchyard abounds with
> images which find a mirror in every mind, and with sentiments
> to which every bosom returns an echo. The four stanzas
> beginning "Yet even these bones" are to me original: I have

never seen the notions in any other place; yet he that reads them here, persuades himself that he has always felt them. Had Gray written often thus, it had been vain to blame, and useless to praise him.

We immediately sense similarities to the previous age — not least in the appeal to 'common sense' — yet already we see the growing development. Vocabulary and sentence structure are far less 'Latinate'. Sentences are still complex, yet here there is a deliberately telling and effective use of balance and contrast. Clauses and phrases are placed with assured fluency and coherence. Consequently, the statements are more effectively highlighted — and nowhere more so than in the (comparatively short) final sentence. Still we note an authorial tone of complete confidence and assurance, yet the whole piece is considerably less formal and academic than the Milton quoted earlier. In such 'conversational' essays, Johnson opened up whole new possibilities for contemplative prose writers.

SUGGESTED FURTHER READING

Fiction:
Jonathan Swift, *Gulliver's Travels*
Henry Fielding, *Tom Jones*
Samuel Richardson, *Pamela*
Tobias Smollett, *Humphrey Clinker*
Daniel Defoe, *Moll Flanders*
Laurence Sterne, *Tristram Shandy*

Non-fiction:
Jonathan Swift, *A Modest Proposal*
James Boswell, *Life of Dr Johnson*
John Locke, *Essay Concerning Human Understanding*
David Hume, *Enquiry Concerning Human Understanding*

ROMANTIC PROSE

Of all our generalizations, this is probably the least satisfactory, as it embraces (from the period of 1760–1830) such diverse works as the Gothic novel, the novels of Sir Walter Scott and Jane Austen and the essays of Lamb, Hazlitt, Shelley and Coleridge. The restless and impassioned

Romantic pre-occupations — the obsession with the individual, Nature, the imagination, death, dreams, the exotic and the mysterious — found their best expression in poetry. Most Romantic prose writing, (for example, the kind found in the Gothic novels, the essays of Hazlitt and in the work of Percy Bysshe Shelley, Mary Shelley and Scott) tends, in itself, to be highly poetic — rich in imagery, metaphor and atmospheric description. The novels of Jane Austen, the most outstanding prose achievements of the age, are, however, more in keeping with the previous age, with an emphasis on civilized behaviour, good taste and humane sanity. These novels displayed the potential of the novel for sharp psychological and social observation, delivered with a most refined sense of irony. The main concerns of Austen's prose are most adequately summarized in one of her own titles — Sense and Sensibility.

The mechanics of style in this age are now more recognizably 'modern'. Here are two examples: the first is from a Gothic novel, Vathek, the second is the celebrated opening of Emma:

a)   The Sultana Dilara, who, till then, had been the favourite, took
this dereliction of the Caliph to heart, with a vehemence natural
to her character; for, during her continuance in favour, she had
imbibed from Vathek many of his extravagant fancies, and was
fired with impatience to behold the superb tombs of Istakhar,
and the palace of forty columns; besides, having been brought
up amongst the Magi, she had fondly cherished the idea of the
Caliph's devoting himself to the worship of fire: thus his
voluptuous and desultory life with her rival was to her a double
source of affliction.

Beckford

b)   Emma Woodhouse, handsome, clever, and rich, with a
comfortable home and happy disposition, seemed to unite some
of the best blessings of existence; and had lived nearly twenty-
one years in the world with very little to distress or vex her.
    She was the youngest of the two daughters of a most
affectionate, indulgent father, and had, in consequence of her
sister's marriage, been mistress of his house from a very early
period. Her mother had died too long ago for her to have more
than an indistinct remembrance of her caresses, and her place
had been supplied by an excellent woman as governess, who had
fallen little short of a mother in affection.

Jane Austen

The Romantic fondness for the exotic is immediately apparent in the first extract, in the use of names if nothing else ("Sultana Dilara", "Caliph", "Vathek", "Magi", "the superb tombs of Istakhar"). The complex sentence is still with us, yet here it is used primarily (and justifiably) to build up the series of mysterious impressions. There is also an emotional quality to the writing (which frequently, in Romantic prose — and here we need only think of a later Romantic classic, *Wuthering Heights* — holds an undercurrent of violence). This emotional quality lies not only in the characters, but also in a feeling that the writer himself is now more 'involved' with his writing. Spelling, grammar and vocabulary now present few problems for the student, who need no longer be intimidated by the passage's initial feeling of strangeness or unfamiliarity, which a modern reader is bound to experience.

In the second passage, we again sense the feeling of authorial detachment. Here the details are employed with balance and precision. The subtle use of balanced statements and pause enable the reader time to 'read between the lines', as it were. This is aided by the delicate use of irony ("*seemed* to unite *some* of the best blessings of existence"). Without stating as much, in so many words, Austen effectively and economically conveys the desired impression of Emma at the opening of the novel — a charming, attractive, probably somewhat superficial and spoiled young lady, with a lot to learn about life.

The student may again have to work a little patiently through sentence structure here, so as not to miss the subtle nuances — something he or she will be unused to doing with the more accessible and familiar structures of modern writing; yet there is little else, by now, of genuine difficulty with 'style'.

SUGGESTED FURTHER READING

Fiction:
Mary Shelley, *Frankenstein*
Jane Austen, *Emma*
Sir Walter Scott, *Ivanhoe*

Non-fiction:
Samuel Coleridge, *Biographia Literaria*
William Hazlitt, *The Spirit of the Age*

VICTORIAN PROSE

This proved the 'Golden Age' of novel writing, not only in England but throughout Europe and in America (and preeminently in Russia). A new outlet was now available to writers trying to live by their writing — serialization of their work in the popular periodicals of the day. This encouraged the growth of the classically long and complex Victorian novel (with their dramatic, "read on next week" chapter endings) that often span several generations (as in Galsworthy's *Forsyte Saga*, or Tolstoy's *War and Peace*). The major dilemma of Victorian society — on the one hand, upright, staid moral certitude (as in the heavy, moralizing essays of Macauley and Carlyle, on the other, growing doubts about religion, industrialization and expanding imperialism — naturally pre-occupies the writers of the time. Dickens writes with a constant eye on social deprivation and abuse. Arnold writes on crises in faith and culture. Newman and Darwin offer psychologically disturbing treatises on religious and philosophic issues. Thackeray explores the class-consciousness of his society and its damaging effects. Emily Bronte probes the psychology of emotional relationships, while George Eliot offers a consummate and comprehensive study of the social, political and historical problems that were unsettling the psychological balance of her contemporaries. A crucial figure, in a pivotal sense, here, is Thomas Hardy. By instinct and style, he looks back to the Romantics and develops the 'poetic' novel to its highest achievement to date. His themes concern the contemporary issues of the dangers of industrialization, social deprivation in rural areas and the invidiously vulnerable position of the Victorian female. Hardy's pessimistic philosophy, however, clearly anticipates the existential and nihilist writing of the mid-twentieth century.

The following two examples are from Thackeray's novel, *Vanity Fair* and Macauley's *Essay on Clive*:

a)   Rawdon opened the door and went in. A little table with a
     dinner was laid out — wine and plate. Steyne was hanging over
     the sofa on which Becky sat. The wretched woman was in
     brilliant full toilette, her arms and all her fingers sparkling with
     bracelets and rings; and the brilliants on her breast which Steyne
     had given her. He had her hand in his, and was bowing over to
     kiss it, when Becky started up with a faint scream as she caught
     sight of Rawdon's white face. At the next instant she tried a
     smile, a horrid smile, as if to welcome her husband: and Steyne
     rose up, grinding his teeth, pale, and with fury in his looks.

                                                        Thackeray

b)   He knew that the standard of morality among the natives of
     India differed widely from that established in England. He knew
     that he had to deal with men destitute of what in Europe is
     called honour, with men who would give any promise without

hesitation, and break any promise without shame, with men who would unscrupulously employ corruption, perjury, forgery to compass their ends. His letters show that the great difference between Asiatic and European morality was constantly in his thoughts. He seems to have imagined, most erroneously in our opinion, that he could effect nothing against such adversaries, if he was content to be bound by ties from which they were free, if he went on telling truth, and hearing none, if he fulfilled, to his own hurt, all his engagements witn confederates who never kept an engagement that was not to their advantage.

Accordingly this man, in the other parts of his life an honourable English gentleman and soldier, was no sooner matched against an Indian intriguer, than he became himself an Indian intriguer, and descended, without scruple, to falsehood, to hypocritical caresses, to the substitution of documents, and to the counterfeiting of hands.

Macauley

There are now few external factors (such as vocabulary, etc) to trouble the modern reader — although one or two words may appear 'old-fashioned' ("toilette", "brilliants", "confederates"). The sentence structure of the second passage still tends to be more elaborate than is common in the more economical 'modern' style (especially the final sentence) and the authorial 'voice' still does not sound like our contemporary writer's — especially in the somewhat pompous (and typically Victorian) Macauley essay ("most erroneously in our opinion"). Yet now, at least, punctuation, grammar and spelling are formalized and totally consistent with our own usage. The novelists, however, are already too diverse to make any meaningful general observations about style. The essayists tend to be more traditional, prizing the virtues of clarity, balance and refinement of the Augustans.

SUGGESTED FURTHER READING

Fiction:
Charles Dickens, *Great Expectations*
Emily Bronte, *Wuthering Heights*
William Thackeray, *Vanity Fair*
George Eliot, *Middlemarch*
Thomas Hardy, *Tess of the d'Urbervilles*

Non-fiction:
Thomas Carlyle, *Sartor Resartus*
Charles Darwin, *Origin of the Species*
Matthew Arnold, *Culture and Anarchy*

Contemporary writing is almost impossible to categorize in any satisfactory way — and, in any case, the student will be far more familiar with such writing. Present century writing — with the explosion in the communications media, its split into 'high' and 'low brow' literature, the proliferation of inexpensive books, magazines and newspapers — has produced a diversity of prose that defies any generalization. Three broad observations will have to suffice. The first two concern primarily 'literary' prose — novels and short stories mainly. The two points to note here are: the element of experimentation with form and structure, as well as style — as in the 'stream of consciousness' techniques of Woolf and Joyce or the structural upheavals of novels such as *Ulysses* or Beckett's *The Unnameable* trilogy — and the increasing interest modern writers have shown in deepening their "psychological" portraits in an attempt to capture the essence of human experience more authentically. The final observation is that the many outlets for serious journalism have ensured a healthy growth in the 'discursive/contemplative' essay.

The gradual movement of twentieth century prose has been away from the specialized, the formal and the "elevated". Writers are more 'familiar', frequently adopting an intimate, or casual, or colloquial "tone". There is less "elitism" about the whole process of prose communication, more a sense of a "man" talking to his fellow "men". In the following examples, I offer, without comment, three extracts. The first is from a typical modern essay by E M Forster 'What I Believe'. The second is Joyce's attempt to reach back and see life through the eyes of a young child from *Portrait of the Artist as a Young Man* and the third by Saul Bellow, is a typically whimsical, clipped, off-beat introduction to a character.

a)   I do not believe in Belief. But this is an age of faith, and there
are so many militant creeds that, in self-defence, one has to
formulate a creed of one's own. Tolerance, good temper and
sympathy are no longer enough in a world which is rent by
religious and racial persecution, in a world where ignorance
rules, and science, who ought to have ruled, plays the
subservient pimp. Tolerance, good temper and sympathy —
they are what matter really, and if the human race is not to
collapse they must come to the front before long. But for the
moment they are not enough, their action is no stronger than a
flower, battered beneath a military jack-boot.

E M Forster

b)   Once upon a time and a very good time it was there was a moocow coming down along the road and this moocow that was down along the road met a nicens little boy named baby tuckoo . . .

His father told him that story: his father looked at him through a glass: he had a hairy face.

He was baby tuckoo. The moocow came down the road where Betty Byrne lived; she sold lemon platt.

O, the wild rose blossoms
On the little green place.

He sang that song. That was his song.

O, the green wothe botheth.

When you wet the bed first it is warm then it gets cold. His mother put on the oilsheet. That had the queer smell.

James Joyce

c)   Papa, poor man, could charm birds from the trees, crocodiles from mud. Madeleine, too, had great charm, and beauty of person also, and a brilliant mind. Valentine Gersbach, her lover, was a charming man, too, though in a heavier, brutal style. He had a thick chin, flaming copper hair that literally gushed from his head (no Thomas Scalp Specialists for him), and he walked on a wooden leg, gracefully bending and straightening like a gondolier.

Saul Bellow

SUGGESTED FURTHER READING

Fiction:

Henry James, *Portrait of a Lady*
Joseph Conrad, *Lord Jim*
Virginia Woolf, *To the Lighthouse*
D H Lawrence, *The Rainbow*
James Joyce, *The Dubliners*
George Orwell, *1984*
Graham Greene, *Power and the Glory*
Ernest Hemingway, *Farewell to Arms*
John Steinbeck, *Of Mice and Men*
Joseph Heller, *Catch 22*

Non-fiction:

E M Forster, *Aspects of the Novel*
D H Lawrence, *Essays*
George Orwell, *Essays*

Reference Passages

As we look at the various elements of prose appreciation — i.e. 'tone', 'rhythm', language', 'style', etc. — the following passages will be used as reference points to give practical application to the general observations made about these elements, to show their usage and potential 'at work' in a given example.

Passage A

I now recalled all the quiet mysteries which I had noted in the man. I remembered that he never spoke but to answer; that, though at intervals he had considerable time to himself, yet I had never seen him reading — no, not even a newspaper; that for long periods he would stand looking out, at his pale window behind the screen, upon the dead brick wall; I was quite sure he never visited any refectory or eating house; that he never went out for a walk; that though so thin and pale, he never complained of ill health. And more than all, I remembered a certain unconscious air of pallid — how shall I call it? — of pallid haughtiness, say, or rather an austere reserve about him, which had positively awed me into my tame compliance with his eccentricities.

As the forlornness of Bartleby grew and grew to my imagination, so did melancholy merge into fear, pity into repulsion. Up to a certain point misery enlists our best affections, but in certain special cases beyond that point it does not. To a sensitive being, pity is not seldom pain. And when at last it is perceived that such pity cannot lead to effectual succour, common sense bids the soul be rid of it. What I saw that morning persuaded me the scrivener* was the victim of an innate and incurable disorder. I might give alms to his body, but it was his soul that suffered, and his soul I could not reach.

Passage B

We came at dusk from the high shallows and saw on a low crest the points of Indian tents, the tepees, and smoke, and silhouettes of tethered horses and blanketed figures moving. In the shadow a rider was following a flock of white goats that flowed like water. The car ran to the top of the crest, and there was a hollow basin with a lake in the distance, pale in the dying

* type of clerk

16

light. And this shallow upland basin, dotted with Indian tents, and the fires flickering in front, and crouching blanketed figures, and horsemen crossing the dusk from tent to tent, horsemen in big steeple hats sitting glued on their ponies, and bells tinkling, and dogs yapping, and tilted wagons trailing in on the trail below, and a smell of wood-smoke and of cooking, and wagons coming in from far off, and tents pricking on the ridge of the round vallum, and horsemen dipping down and emerging again, and more red sparks of fires glittering, and crouching bundles of women's figures squatting at a fire before a little tent made of boughs, and little girls in full petticoats hovering, and wild barefoot boys throwing bones at thin-tailed dogs, and tents away in the distance, in the growing dark, on the slopes, and the trail crossing the floor of the hollows in the low dusk.

There you had it all, as in the hollow of your hand. And to my heart, born in England and kindled with Fenimore Cooper, it wasn't the wild and woolly West, it was the nomad nations gathering still in the continent of hemlock trees and prairies. The Apaches came and talked to us, in their steeple black hats and plaits wrapped with beaver fur, and their silver beads and turquoise. Some talked strong American, and some talked only Spanish. And they had strange lines in their faces.

Passage C

I cannot praise a fugitive and cloistered virtue, unexercised and un-breathed, that never sallies out and sees her adversary, but slinks out of the race, where that immortal garland is to be run for, not without dust and heat. Assuredly we bring not innocence into the world, we bring impurity much rather; that which purifies us is trial, and trial is by what is contrary. That virtue therefore which is but a youngling in the contemplation of evil, and knows not the utmost that vice promises to her followers, and rejects it, is but a blank virtue, not a pure; her whiteness is but an excremental whiteness. Which was the reason why our sage and serious poet Spenser, whom I dare be known to think a better teacher than Scotus or Aquinas, describing true temperance under the person of Guion, brings him in with his palmer through the cave of Mammon, and the bower of earthly bliss, that he might see and know, and yet abstain. Since therefore the knowledge and survey of vice is in this world so necessary to the constituting of human virtue, and the scanning of error to the confirmation of truth, how can we more safely, and with less danger, scout into the regions of sin and falsity than by reading all manner of tracts and hearing all manner of reason? And this is the benefit which may be had of books promiscuously read.

CHAPTER 3

WORDS, WORDS, WORDS

TWO TYPES OF READING

The first, and obvious, objective when confronting a piece of prose is to determine what the passage is about. Just as there is an 'art' to reading poetry for the purpose of analysis, so it is with prose — an 'art' that is not achieved magically during late revision, but one that is only gradually acquired and developed through constant practice. The student who has read a wide variety of poetry during the course will clearly be in a stronger position than a student who has 'tolerated' the bare minimum. Extended background reading is even more important when it comes to prose appreciation. Breadth of vocabulary, familiarity with unusual or complex ideas, acquaintance with different styles and periods of writing — as well as an increasing sophistication in one's own ideas and ability to express them — none of these are achieved overnight. For overseas students of English Literature (i.e. the type of student who is not constantly immersed in the sort of 'native' English writers will inevitably use) they are the very areas that need most conscious development. The simple fact for any student of English Literature is that one can never read too much.

All types of reading — novels, stories, essays, articles, etc. — will provide a wealth of background for the student to draw upon. Comparisons and contrasts with background reading will help to highlight the specific qualities of any passage before him. Relevant parallels and cross-references will not only help to make any analysis more complete but will also give an indication of how the student has approached his course in general.

Of more immediate importance, however, will be the 'quality' of reading; that is, the amount of concentration and sensitivity the student is able to bring to his reading of a given set passage. It is amazing how often students fail to read the instructions that accompany examination questions, even at university level. The slant of Advanced Level examination questions varies slightly from year to year — yet two instructions remain constant. The first advises the student to *read carefully* the given passage, and the second to analyse with *close reference* to the passage itself.

It is all too easy (and perfectly understandable) for students to allow examination pressure and tension to rush them into an inadequately prepared analysis. The student feels he is being assessed on what he writes, so the sooner he begins writing (and the more he writes, many mistakenly suppose) the sooner he will begin gaining marks and credit. Yet Poetry and Prose Appreciation questions are as much (if not more) an assessment of the student's ability to *read* accurately and sensitively as they are of his ability to write. Examiners of such examinations constantly bemoan the fact that enough time is not taken by students over their *reading* — a fact which tends to produce a plethora of shallow and repetitive analyses. Quite simply, the quality of a student's written analysis will depend entirely on the 'quality' of his reading.

BASIC COMPREHENSION

The student will need to take as long as necessary over his readings of a passage, so that he begins to acquire a basic grasp of what the passage is trying to achieve. Hasty, random, superficial observations will hardly constitute the type of analysis the examiner is seeking. Certain obstacles may well delay a student's initial efforts to comprehend the passage. The most likely of these are:

Vocabulary The appearance of unfamiliar words frequently dismays students, causing many, inwardly, to 'give up' on the passage and merely make a token or dispirited attempt at analysis. There are two aspects to the problem of vocabulary. Firstly, if the type of word causing problems can be reasonably expected to be within the vocabulary range of an Advanced Level English student (i.e. 'dichotomy', 'ocular', *'laissez-faire'*, etc.), then it is the student's own approach to the course (in terms of background reading, vocabulary extension, etc.) that is at fault and little can be done to remedy this in examination time. Secondly, if the vocabulary is at times highly specialized or sophisticated (and perhaps beyond the student's expected range), there will be other areas of the passage that will enable the

19

student to acquire a broad grasp of what is being said — that will define, develop or modify the main ideas in simpler terms. It is important to avoid 'examination panic' and to keep working at the passage. The examiner is not trying to trick students, or 'catch them out'. He simply wants an example of the sort of work the student is capable of to assess the sort of standard that has been reached.

Particularly obscure, or technical, or foreign terms will generally be explained by means of footnotes.

Unfamiliar and Complex Concepts   Any passage containing difficult concepts will not do so merely for the sake of it (the passage is badly written if this is the case). It will do so because such things cannot be said otherwise without distorting over-simplification. Such complex sections of the passage will develop naturally from the general flow of ideas being discussed. Once again, calm, concentrated and continued reading will lead the student to the heart of the passage. A successful student on this type of course will, with practice, develop the *confidence* to realize that no passage set in any such examination will be beyond his capabilities and will also have developed the *patience* to approach such passages in the correct manner. He will then be in a position to distinguish between a passage that is complex because the *writer* himself is not clear or sure and a passage that is complex because the *issue* is not clear or simple.

Syntax   Again, there are two likely problems. If the subject-matter of a passage is dense and complex, then, in order to accommodate such expression adequately, grammatical structures will involve a complicated series of subjunctives and inter-related clause patterns. Comprehension will only come through following the thought-process through the necessary grammatical sophistication. It should be remembered (if only for the comfort it brings) that a writer's main aim is to be understood as fully as possible. Unlike a 'speaker', a writer cannot be halted and questioned as to his meaning. He must therefore be as precise as his subject allows. He does not seek to be 'clever' by using obscure, confusing sentence structures — rather the opposite. Grammatical links and structuring may be a further problem if the writer is attempting 'interior monologue', or 'stream of consciousness', or 'poetic' prose. There will be no insurmountable problems, however, that proper preparation and careful reading will not unravel.

The other type of syntax problem may relate to passages written before the twentieth-century. The entire passage may appear unfamiliar and alien — perhaps un-English. Yet such differences as are likely — in terms of spelling, punctuation, or grammatical structuring — are really only surface difficulties. Such passages, more than any others, will call upon previous reading, exposure to different "eras" of prose writing and wide-ranging practice. If necessary, a little initiative and imagination will help clarify minor obscurities.

Unfamiliar Situations, Events, Characters   This should prove much less of a problem. The passage may be exclusively concerned with experiences completely beyond those of the student. Yet such cultural, social or geographical unfamiliarity will present no real problem to the sensitive reader. Indeed, one of the joys of reading is to expand our awareness of things we may never personally experience and to share them (albeit on a 'second-hand' basis) with someone who has. An anthropological account of eskimos is not beyond the 'appreciative' scope of a reader in the Tropics, any more than a passage dealing with, say, the death of a son, is beyond the imaginative and emotional grasp of a sixteen year-old.

COMPREHENSION AND THE REFERENCE PASSAGES

Passage A

Here we may say that the writer is concerned with giving the narrator's reaction to the strange character 'Bartleby'. The first paragraph deals with the ways in which Bartleby is different or unusual from others of the narrator's acquaintance and experience. The second paragraph looks in greater detail at the narrator's specific and changing attitude towards such a seemingly mysterious and sad figure.

Passage B

In this passage the author provides a first-hand account of his first acquaintance with modern-day Red Indians. He offers considerable and atmospheric detail about their encampment and indicates that the experience presents a reality that differed greatly from what he had been led to expect from his reading of the 'wild West'.

Passage C

Here the author is defining what he considers to be true 'virtue'. His basic argument is that 'virtue' does not lie in an innocence and purity that detaches itself from the world and its trials, but more in actually confronting evil, subjecting itself to temptation and then rising above it. The argument moves towards a justification for allowing open access to all types of books, even those that are potentially morally harmful, so that 'virtue' is not shielded and protected from vice, but rather proves itself in facing vice squarely and refusing to succumb.

It can be seen from the above, that in dealing with basic comprehension we need do no more than give the broadest summary. This is to direct the later analysis and also to indicate to the examiner that one has a sound grasp of the basic situation or argument of the passage. To ensure this is done, examiners on this paper have increasingly taken to setting an opening question that asks the candidate to give just such an outline of the passage's situation, characters, events or argument.

Exercises

1. What is the highest of all the goods which are the objects of action? So far as the name goes, there is a pretty general agreement: for HAPPINESS both the multitude and the refined few call it, and "living well" and "doing well" they conceive to be the same with "being happy"; but about the Nature of this Happiness, men dispute, and the multitude do not in their account of it agree with the wise. For some say it is some one of those things which are palpable and apparent, as pleasure or wealth or honour; in fact, some one thing, some another; nay, oftentimes the same man gives a different account of it; for when ill, he calls it health; when poor, wealth: and conscious of their own ignorance, men admire those who talk grandly and above their comprehension. Some again hold it to be something by itself, other than and beside these many good things, which is in fact to all these the cause of their being good.

   a. What is the author attempting to define in this extract?
   b. What difficulties prevent him from achieving a clear, simple definition?

2. Religions may be divided into those that are political and those that concern the individual soul. Confucianism is a political religion: Confucius, as he wandered from court to court, became concerned essentially with the problem of government, and with the instilling of such

virtues as to make good government easy. Buddhism, in spite of the fact that in its early days it was the religion of princes, is essentially non-political. I do not mean it has always remained so. In Tibet it is as political as the papacy . . . Nevertheless, the Buddhist, in his more religious moments, considers himself essentially as a solitary being. Islam, on the contrary, was from its very beginning a political religion. Mahomet made himself a ruler of men, and the caliphs who succeeded him remained so until the conclusion of the Great War. It is typical of the difference between Islam and Christianity that the caliph combined within himself both temporal and spiritual authority, which to a Mahometan are not distinct; whereas Christianity, by its non-political character, was led to create two rival politicians, namely, the Pope and the Emperor.

a. What general argument does the author offer concerning religion and politics?

b. How does the author specifically differentiate between Islam and Christianity?

3. Why then did Benjamin set up this dummy of a perfect citizen as a pattern to America? Of course, he did it in perfect good faith, as far as he knew. He thought it simply was the true ideal. But what we *think* we do is not very important. We never really know what we are doing. Either we are materialistic instruments, like Benjamin, or we move in the gesture of creation, from our deepest self, usually unconscious. We are only the actors, we are never wholly the authors of our own deeds or works.

a. The writer has been attacking Benjamin Franklin's description of the 'perfect citizen'. What is the basis for the author thinking such a creation of a 'perfect pattern' is futile?

CHAPTER 4

TYPES OF PROSE

Unlike poetry, prose does not fall into neatly defined forms such as sonnets, blank verse, etc. We must therefore look at the 'type' of prose and consider its function or objective — i.e. to inform, to describe, to change, etc. Assessing the type of prose serves a limited, yet useful purpose; limited because many passages will combine different 'types' of prose writing simultaneously, yet useful in providing a starting-point that will direct the more detailed analysis to follow. The different types of prose fall into the following broad categories.

NARRATIVE

This is the most common type of prose found in novels and stories. Basically it relates to any sort of writing that tells a story, or develops a plot. If a given extract deals with events or situations, they are likely to be those of a particularly telling or significant nature (for the characters or the author); if it deals with a character, it will illuminate something important about that character in action. In narrative prose, the writer is concerned with two basic objectives:

1. to give the reader all the necessary and relevant information so that characters and events in his narrative are explained, or make sense;

2. to promote and sustain the reader's interest and curiosity, offering the interesting, the unusual, or the intriguing in character and situation.

The second aspect will be in particular evidence at the beginning of a work, while in the same way a sense of drama or suspense often accompanies passages that close a chapter or section.

Narrative prose will be either *first* or *third person* narrative. The first person, or 'I' narrative generally produces a more personal, intimate form of communication. The reader is drawn in to share the writer's experience and a sense of sympathy or understanding is frequently developed, even when the narrator is seen to transgress moral or legal norms — as in Nabakov's 'Lolita'. The third person narrative is more 'detached', yet its scope is wider. The writer (and the reader following him) assumes a 'godlike' perspective above the action, showing us all things at all times and leading us into the minds and hearts and motives of all his main characters.

There is also a type of narrative prose known as 'stream of consciousness'. This is a modern development (although Sterne experimented with such an idea back in the eighteenth-century) that seeks to take the first person narrative even deeper. The aim is to reproduce the random flow of frequently unassociated ideas that race through the human mind at any given moment. The objective, external world is diminished and everything is seen exclusively through the perceptions of one mind, which is analysed in all its ramifications, with the trivial and the significant side by side. It is an attempt to be more accurate and honest in the portrayal of human psychology. Some find the technique claustrophobic and its linguistic convolutions that attempt to express 'thought in action' trying (as many exponents of this technique will do away with punctuation altogether — arguing that we do not 'think' with punctuation). Nevertheless, in the hands of a Joyce or a Woolf, it has proved an extremely effective form of narration.

DESCRIPTIVE

Here the main function, obviously, is to describe, to give as accurately, or intriguingly, or powerfully as possible a deep impression of a character, place, or situation. The reader should 'feel' the scene and be able to see it or hear it as vividly as possible. Such prose is usually strong on atmosphere and the atmosphere of the description will say much about how the writer, or the characters involved, feel about what is being described. Such writing is usually the sort of prose that assumes a 'poetic' quality and will employ images and figurative language to colour the descriptions and involve the reader's emotions.

Novels and stories will generally combine narrative and descriptive prose in the flow of the writing, even within short extracts. An event may be narrated, followed by a description of the mood or feeling it produces in the characters.

The effective use of *detail* is crucial to good descriptive writing. A writer cannot include everything about a person or an event, so he will seek the most telling and significant details, those that give us the very essence of the person, place, or event as he sees them. The type of detail chosen and the sort of associations aroused will say much about how the writer feels towards his subject; we always, for instance, know exactly how Dickens feels (and wants the reader to feel) about all his characters from his initial descriptions.

The student should consider the use of detail carefully. Does the writer have a real 'eye' for telling detail? Do the details combine to produce a uniform atmosphere? Are they surprising, unexpected, memorable? Do the details come alive for the reader and allow him to visualize or understand more vividly? Or are the details perhaps contrived or stale or insignificant?

DISCURSIVE

Discursive writing offers the writer's thoughts on a·particular topic, such as 'the delights of living in the country', or 'the tribulations of urban life', providing general observations from his own personal, and perhaps humorous or unusual, perspective. There is usually a sense of a mind enjoying its own intellectual activity and creative expression. The basic intention will vary somewhat, as the word 'discourse' can mean a lecture or sermon, whereas 'discursive' has connotations of random observations and light conversation. A novelist may well employ discursive sections to reveal the thoughts and values of his characters — a more subtle means of 'characterization' than simply telling us how characters think and feel, as the reader shares the actual thoughts.

CONTEMPLATIVE

This is similar to discursive but is worth differentiating as the level of 'contemplation' is deeper and more serious. We are given a more profound insight into the writer's thoughts and a clearer grasp of how he feels and why. The subject matter will be more serious than that of 'discursive' prose. Essays and the more serious forms of journalism are frequently 'contemplative'. A novelist may also use 'contemplative' prose in those sections of the narrative where a character is considering a dilemma, a choice, or brooding over a potentially perilous course of action (such as we find with Raskolnikov in *Crime and Punishment*).

PHILOSOPHIC

If a passage talks of the simple delights of an early morning walk in spring through a forest it is *discursive*. If this leads into the deeper thoughts and reactions of the writer, about the environment, or his life, it will become *contemplative*. If it proceeds to consider the relationship between Man and Nature, it becomes *philosophic*. This form of writing is more 'formal' and structured than the previous two, where a specific topic of philosophy, religion, or politics (to name only the more obvious ones) will be analysed and 'debated'. Such writing will generally work towards a particular 'thesis', or belief, which the writing itself will support.

Given the increased seriousness of subject-matter from the previous two types of prose, the tone and language are likely to be more elevated and complex. Such writing is most likely to come from the specialized text or essay. It is important to realize that we are talking here about a phi-losophic mode of writing and not a writer's actual philosophy — i.e. his values and beliefs. In novels, for instance, the writer's philosophy is more likely to be *implied* by the work as a whole rather than stated outright.

DIDACTIC/DIRECTIVE

Such writing attempts to influence the reader's thinking or behaviour in a specific manner, as the writer seeks to persuade, or cajole, or coerce the reader into thinking in a certain way. Generally, such writing deals with moral or political issues and is most commonly found in the sermon, treatise, journalism, or, at its lowest form, propaganda. The writer is usually passionately involved with his subject, seeing wrongs and evils that must be corrected. At its best, such writing can be powerful, moving and persuasive (as in the sermons of John Donne). At its worst, it usually reeks of fanaticism and, though its social consequences may be dangerous, it is usually poor writing.

A differentiation may be made between 'didactic' and 'directive'. At a simple level, it lies in the difference between the impassioned prose of a sermon and the detached prose of instruction (which 'directs' the reader as to what to do). *Didactic* is, in fact, best reserved for purely moral issues, while *directive* adequately covers the rest.

SATIRIC

Like certain other literary terms — i.e. 'pathetic' — the modern usage of this word does not fully indicate the original meaning. Nowadays, we tend to use the word 'satiric' for anything that ridicules the excesses or pretensions of certain types of people (politicians being an ever-popular target, especially for cartoonists). Traditionally, however, a 'satire' was more seriously intended and conceived. It highlighted folly, immorality or excess by exaggeration, thereby deflating it and making it appear ludicrous and ridiculous. Yet such satires had the genuinely didactic purpose of correcting such weaknesses, or at least preventing those possessed of them from gaining power and influence. The hope was that the reader would note the ludicrous, despicable and contemptible nature of such behaviour and avoid it himself — if only for fear of appearing equally ridiculous.

The elements of satire tend to be exaggeration, disproportion, ridicule and sarcasm. The reader must catch the right tone to avoid a reading that is too literal and taken at face value — the type of reading that might dismiss *Animal Farm* as a harmless fantasy of 'talking' animals. Modern satire has tended to be less moral than traditional satire, highlighting folly, etc. in an anarchic or destructive manner without offering or implying an alternative — as in the 'Absurd' dramatists.

PROSE 'TYPES' AND THE REFERENCE PASSAGES

Passage A

Here we have a basically *descriptive* piece of prose, where the writer describes the idiosyncracies of the character Bartleby and the effect they produce on the narrator. There is a slight shift in the 'type' of prose between the two paragraphs. The first is concerned only with describing the behaviour of Bartleby. The second, however, becomes more *contemplative* as we are given the narrator's inner reaction. It is contemplative rather than, say, discursive, because the writer is not simply offering random observation. Obviously the narrator has considered the problem of a person like Bartleby quite deeply and even goes on to speculate about 'human sympathy' in general.

Passage B

This passage is more purely *descriptive*, as the author is at pains to give a vivid and realistic impression of his first encounter with the Apaches. A broad, panoramic canvas is offered, dense with specific details and images, as the richly atmospheric scene evolves. The opening observation of the second paragraph indicates how unexpected such a scene was for the author — and the entire 'slant' of the descriptions is aimed at conveying this element of the unexpected and providing a powerful evocation of how the modern Apaches really live.

Passage C

As this passage is concerned with an area of moral philosophy — i.e. the true nature of 'virtue' — and as the author works towards clearly defined conclusions (rather than simply 'offering' possible ideas and observations) we can see the passage as being *philosophic*. It is somewhat unusual for such writing, as it seeks to make a more memorable impression by 'poetically' translating abstract concepts such as virtue and vice, into objects of personification and seeing their conflicts, etc. in terms of images and metaphors.

Exercises

1. There remained only the last water-jump, a yard and a half across. Vronsky did not even look at it but, anxious to get in first by a long way, began sawing on the reins with a circular movement, raising the mare's head and letting it go in time with her stride. He felt she was using her last reserve of strength; not merely her neck and shoulders were wet, but on her mane, her head, her pointed ears the sweat stood out in drops and her breath came in short, harsh gasps. But he knew

that her reserve of strength was more than enough for the remaining five hundred yards. Only because he felt himself nearer the ground and by the peculiar smoothness of her motion did Vronsky know how greatly the mare had increased her pace. She cleared the ditch as if she did not notice it, flying over like a bird; but at that very instant Vronsky, to his horror, felt that, instead of keeping up with the mare's pace, for some inexplicable reason he had made a dreadful, unforgivable blunder and dropped back into the saddle. All at once his position had shifted and he knew that something terrible had happened.

a. What type of prose is this?
b. By what means does the writer attempt to achieve a sense of realism and drama?
c. Does the writer effectively convey a vivid impression of the rider and horse involved in the race? If so, how?

2. The likings and dislikings of society, or of some powerful portion of it, are thus the main thing which has practically determined the rules laid down for general observance, under the penalties of law and opinion. And in general, those who have been in advance of society in thought and feeling, have left this condition of things unassailed in principle, however they may have come into conflict with it in some of its details. They have occupied themselves rather in inquiring what things society ought to like or dislike, than in questioning whether its likings or dislikings should be a law to individuals.

a. How would you describe this type of prose?
b. What basic point is the author seeking to establish?

3. The man drowsed off into what seemed to him the most comfortable and satisfying sleep he had ever known. The dog sat facing him and waiting. The brief day drew to a close in a long, slow twilight. There were no signs of a fire to be made, and, besides, never in the dog's experience had it known a man to sit like that in the snow and make no fire. As the twilight drew on, its eager yearning for the fire mastered it, and with a great lifting and shifting of forefeet, it whined softly, then flattened its ears down in anticipation of being chided by the man. But the man remained silent. Later, the dog whined loudly. And still later it crept close to the man and caught the scent of death. This made the animal bristle and back away. A little longer it delayed, howling under the stars that leaped and danced and shone brightly in the cold sky. Then it turned and trotted up the trail in the direction of the camp it knew, where were the other food providers and fire providers.

a. What type of prose is this?
b. Which details give the passage its most vivid impact?
c. Do you find this handling of a death-scene effective?

4. Master Pangloss taught the metaphysico-theologo-cosmolo-nigology. He could prove to admiration that there is no effect without a cause; and that, in the best of all possible worlds, the Baron's castle was the most magnificent of all castles, and my lady the best of all possible baronesses.

"It is demonstrable", he said, "that things cannot be otherwise than they are; for as all things have been created for some end, they must necessarily be created for the best end. Observe, for instance, the nose is formed for spectacles, therefore we wear spectacles. The legs are visibly designed for stockings, accordingly we wear stockings . . ."

a. This passage is intended satirically. What is the object of the writer's satiric 'attack'?
b. How does the passage achieve its satiric intention?

5. . . . only a quarter after what an unearthly hour I suppose they're just getting up in China now combing out their pigtails for the day well soon have the nuns ringing the angelus they've nobody coming in to spoil their sleep except an old priest or two for his night office the alarm clock next door clattering the brains out of itself let me see if I can doze off 1 2 3 4 5 what kind of flowers are those they invented like the stars the wallpaper in Lombard street was much nicer the apron he gave me was something like that . . .

a. This type of narrative is called 'stream of consciousness'. What is the author trying to achieve in such a passage?
b. Do you find such writing effective?
c. Comment on the absence of punctuation and its effect?

CHAPTER 5

TONE

Frequently, the *tone* in which something is said is more significant than the actual words being used, in terms of what the speaker really intends to convey. A disgruntled teacher returning an extremely poor assignment to a student with a sarcastic "Marvellous" — intends the exact opposite of the word being used. It is the tone that would register the necessary dissatisfaction and, perhaps, anger. In prose appreciation, if we are to perceive how the writer feels about what he is writing (and how he wishes the reader to feel), it is essential that we grasp the 'tone' accurately.

Tone can refer to the 'tone' the writer adopts towards his reader, as well as the 'tone' in which he delivers his material. If we can accurately gauge a writer's tone we begin to sense the writer's true feelings and therefore we are in a better position to assess the intention behind a given passage. We may describe tone by using any of the adjectives we might use for 'tone of voice'. The writer may be aggressive, or humble, or confiding towards the reader. In the actual writing, the subject-matter may be presented in a wistful, or admiring, or harsh, or colloquial tone.

The student should imagine the writer himself reading the passage. What tone, the student should ask, would be detected in his voice? Is the tone consistent throughout a passage, or does it shift and change, as if the writer has suddenly thought of something else, or has been leading the reader one way to turn him round another? Any such changes in tone (and observations as to why they have been introduced) will again be invaluable in the assessment of the writer's purpose.

TONE AND ATMOSPHERE

These two elements are frequently confused by students, yet they are quite distinct. *Atmosphere* describes the prevailing mood of a passage, an attempt by the writer to make the reader react, or feel, in a certain way. *Tone* tells us how the writer already feels about his subject. The two are closely related and usually similar. If the tone of a passage is wistful and yearning, the prevailing atmosphere will probably be sad and melancholic, perhaps nostalgic. Atmosphere, however, is related more to the emotive words the passage may use (i.e. those words designed to provoke an emotional response). It will be related more specifically to the descriptive sections of a passage, especially those containing images and metaphors.

I have said that tone and atmosphere are frequently similar. This need not always be the case. A passage may adopt a 'light-hearted' tone in its treatment of tragic or sad material — an unexpected device that often achieves the desired effect of actually deepening the underlying feeling, or atmosphere of tragic pathos. (We see this, for instance, at the end of Hardy's *Tess of the D'Urbervilles* where the heroine's hopeless and inevitable destruction is almost 'casually' dismissed with: "Justice was done, and the President of the Immortals, in Aeschylean phrase, had ended his sport with Tess".) The basic point about tone and atmosphere is that they should work together, complementing each other — like different sections of an orchestra, each playing their different parts for the harmonious, overall effect.

TONE AND IRONY

Most mis-readings of passages are attributable to a student's missing of the intended tone — taking a light-hearted, tongue-in-cheek piece too seriously and literally, or a missing of the deeper implications of a seemingly non-serious, or trivial passage. (One recalls the bishop who, upon reading *Gulliver's Travels*, confessed he liked the style of the narrative but found the story a trifle 'improbable and far-fetched'!)

The main problem here is most likely to stem from the author's use of *irony*. Irony is an extremely subtle device. At its simplest level, it means *stating* one thing, but *meaning* something else (often the opposite) — as in sarcasm. The writer may seek, in this manner, to convey his real intentions through irony. In a sense, irony is the opposite of direct statement and writers often feel that direct statements will appear too simplistic, or unre-fined, or even obvious, to achieve a profound effect. Irony forces us to think more, perhaps to "read between the lines" for what is *not* being said, to sense the unstated implications. We may, at this point, look again at a passage already quoted from Jane Austen's opening description of Emma:

> Emma Woodhouse, handsome, clever, and rich, with a
> comfortable home and happy disposition, seemed to unite some
> of the best blessings of existence; and had lived nearly twenty-
> one years in the world with very little to distress or vex her.

This is an important passage, as it is the reader's introduction to the main character of the novel. The statements *appear* almost entirely positive and complimentary, yet there is a constant use of subtle irony throughout the passage which, even on first reading, expands the simple surface portrait with deeper implications. Emma is "handsome" and "clever" (as opposed, we feel, to "beautiful" and "intelligent"). Other touches, "comfortable", "with very little to distress or vex her", gently suggest a character who has never experienced the harshness of real life, perhaps even a pampered smugness. It is difficult to miss the irony in "seemed" and "some" in "seemed to unite some of the best blessings of existence".

When irony is handled with the gentle subtlety of a Jane Austen, it is easy to see how readers may sometimes miss the point — especially in a short extract. Other instances will be more obvious. If a passage appears extreme, or inconsistent, or simply does not feel right, the student should mentally pose certain questions. Is it likely that the writer (or anyone, for that matter) could really believe what he is actually saying? Does this sound like the writer's 'real voice', or could he be adopting a particular 'tone' to create certain impressions? Could a more serious meaning lie behind a seemingly absurd, extreme, or irreverent passage? Is the heavy seriousness of a passage overdone — and perhaps mocking those who do think and argue in such a manner? Is the writer deliberately teasing, or misleading, or challenging the reader — and, if so, why?

Irony is especially evident in satiric writing — yet the 'ironic mode', where a writer self-effacingly observes his own shortcomings (and those of others), has become popular with contemporary novelists and essayists. However, the student should take care not to read too much into a passage, i.e. see irony where it was never intended. Some students fre-quently resort to this opposite extreme as a corrective to previous passages where they have initially missed deeper implications. Even with this danger in mind, it is always worth the student's trouble to ask whether a passage could mean something other than the student's own inter-pretation.

TONE AND THE REFERENCE PASSAGES

Passage A

The tone of the opening paragraph suggests bewilderment, confusion, even a slight sense of disbelief and wonder, as the narrator attempts to analyse Bartleby's behaviour and character. This is conveyed largely by the long second sentence, where each unusual aspect of Bartleby's character is simply listed without any possible explanation. The tone of the opening paragraph is probably best captured in the narrator's confession of his inability to describe Bartleby accurately when he asks "how shall I call it?"

The tone of the second paragraph reveals a decrease in the frustration at not being able to 'reach' Bartleby in any meaningful way. The attitude hardens and the pity diminishes, as the narrator tries to account for his changing feelings by abstract and detached observations about human nature in general.

Passage B

Tone and atmosphere play a significant role in this passage. The tone is hushed, with a slight sense of surprise, perhaps even awe. We feel the scene has totally taken over the writer's consciousness and the long accumulation of detail, with the constant use of 'and' almost produces the effect of an incantation. Complementing this is the dream-like atmosphere, as the shadowy, indeterminate scene is slowly conjured before us. A feeling of silence pervades the entire scene — emphasized all the more by the occasional sounds (bells tinkling, dogs yapping, the Apaches speaking). The atmosphere of dusk — in itself a slightly mysterious time of melting colours, shifting perspectives and growing dark — is perfectly captured and intensified by the blanketed figures and flickering fires. Because the scene has so surprised the writer — in terms of his pre-conceived expectations — the encampment seems alien and unreal.

Passage C

The confident, assertive tone of this passage is evident from the opening statement — "I cannot praise . . ." and is maintained throughout ("Assuredly we bring not . . . ", "whom I dare to be known to think . . ."). We sense here a mind that feels it has weighed the matter before it and has arrived at conclusions that are completely sound and firm. The passage proceeds on a 'step by step' basis to confirm its argument — "Since therefore . . .", "how can we more safely . . ." — an argument which the author's slightly aggressive attitude clearly feels there is no contradicting. The final statement concludes the passage appropriately with its sense of conviction, although some readers may find it somewhat smug — perhaps even dogmatic and domineering.

Exercises

1. It is the observation of some ancient sage, whose name I have forgot, that passions operate differently on the human mind, as diseases on the body, in proportion to the strength or weakness, soundness or rottenness, of the one and the other.

    We hope, therefore, a judicious reader will give himself some pains to observe, what we have so greatly laboured to describe, the different operations of this passion of love in the gentle and cultivated mind of the Lady Booby, from those which it effected in the less polished and coarser disposition of Mrs Slipslop.

    a. How would you describe the tone of such writing?
    b. What tone, or attitude, does the author adopt towards the reader?

2. They were now approaching the cottage, and all idle topics were superseded. Emma was very compassionate; and the distresses of the poor were as sure of relief from her personal attention and kindness, her counsel and her patience, as from her purse. She understood their ways, could allow for their ignorance and their temptations, had no romantic expectations of extraordinary virtue from those, for whom education had done so little; entered into their troubles with ready sympathy, and always gave her assistance with as much intelligence as goodwill. In the present instance, it was sickness and poverty together which she came to visit.

    a. Is there anything in the author's underlying tone here that casts doubts on the motives behind Emma's charity?

3. Fog everywhere. Fog up the river, where it flows among green aits and meadows; fog down the river, where it rolls defiled among the tiers of shipping, and the waterside pollutions of a great (and dirty) city. Fog on the Essex Marshes, fog on the Kentish heights. Fog creeping into the cabooses of collier-brigs; fog lying out on the yards, and hovering

in the rigging of great ships; fog drooping on the gunwales of barges and small boats. Fog in the eyes and throats of ancient Greenwich pensioners, wheezing by the firesides of their wards . . .

a. How would you describe the tone of this extract?
b. The passage falls at the opening of a novel. What is the atmosphere and feeling being established here?

CHAPTER 6

RHYTHM

Rhythm in prose refers to the general way in which a passage moves and flows. Again it will depend on the effect that is being sought. If a passage is concerned with expressing serious or complex ideas, it will move at a steady, balanced rate. Descriptive prose, generally, will also accumulate its details in a sure and firm manner, so that nothing of the general effect is lost — unless what is being described is particularly exciting or breathtaking, when it will seek effects of pause and climax as appropriate. Narrative prose will usually offer the greatest variety of rhythmic effects, where the pace may be quickened — through dialogue, or short sentences and paragraphs — to increase the sense of drama, or considerably slowed down to build up suspense.

The key to observing the rhythm lies in the sentence and paragraph structuring. Long sentences and paragraphs move much more slowly than shorter ones — which are capable of producing genuine effects of drama (many a chapter ends with a short, one-sentence paragraph). 'Dramatic' punctuation — exclamations, questions, etc. — will also effect the rhythm, producing either a quickening of pace, or a broken, staccato impact.

As with all aspects of prose appreciation, such generalized statements only serve as useful guidelines; the student will always have to assess the specific effects before him in a given passage.

Rhythm And The Reference Passages

Passage A

The passage opens with a short, arresting sentence that arouses our interest in what is to follow. The second sentence — an extremely long and complex one — accumulates details of Bartleby in separate segments, isolated by the extensive use of the semi-colon. The effect gradually builds up and quickens, to convey the narrator's sense of confusion — aided by more dramatic punctuation such as dashes and questions. The second paragraph moves with more balance and control, as the narrator resigns himself to not being able to help Bartleby. The rhythm is more steady and regular as the narrator ceases to allow himself to be upset or frustrated by Bartleby. This steady balance and control is best displayed in the final sentence.

Passage B

The rhythm of this passage is more akin to that of poetry than prose. This is best typified by the exceptionally long sentence that closes the first paragraph. Here there is a steady flow to the movement, as the impressions are mounted one on top of the other. The author uses an abundance of commas — which act almost as verse line-endings and do not break the flow of description as a full-stop or semi-colon would — and constant repetition of "and" as we move smoothly from one detail to another. This is very much in keeping with the writer's purpose. He does not want us to perceive random details, but, as far as possible, wants to create in the reader the impression of viewing the scene, at one glance, in its panoramic entirety — as we would with a painting. This intricate, flowing rhythm suggests the way in which all the details form an integral, coherent part of the whole scene. Taken out of its context, such a sentence would appear crudely and simplistically written — almost like that of a child lacking grammatical sophistication — yet here we are swayed by movement until, like the author himself (and this is the impression he is trying to communicate) we 'watch' the scene in 'trance-like' captivation. This opening paragraph also closes with an effectively gentle, 'falling away' movement as we look out at the trail.

The second paragraph opens with a more direct and halting movement, as the author describes his reaction. Yet the description of the Apaches that closes the passage returns to the gentle rhythmic patterns (with more commas and 'ands') of the first paragraph.

The basic rhythm that we have noted in this passage is very much in harmony with the element of 'incantation' we saw in the tone.

Passage C

The comma is also used to good effect in this passage as the sentences are again long and elaborate. The basic movement here is steady and controlled, in keeping with the serious subject matter. This balance and control is evident in nearly all the sentences, especially one such as:

> Assuredly we bring not innocence into the world, we bring
> impurity much rather; that which purifies us is trial, and trial is
> by what is contrary.

The sentence is balanced by the mid-point semi-colon and the two 'sub-divisions' balanced, at an almost exact mid-point again, by a comma. The longer sentence containing the allusion to Spenser builds decisively to the climax held in the short final phrase "and yet abstain". This serves to emphasize the writer's point all the more. Similarly, the shortest sentence falls right at the end of the passage to conclude on a note of conviction and finality. This steady, assured rhythm suggests to the reader that the writer is 'in command' and has thought long and deeply about his subject and can be 'trusted' or at least listened to with respect.

Exercises

1. The ringing of bells, the surging and swelling of bells supra urbem*, above the whole city, in its airs overfilled with sound. Bells, bells, they swing and sway, they wag and weave through their whole arc on their beams, in their seats, hundred-voiced, in Babylonish confusion. Slow and swift, blaring and booming — there is neither measure nor harmony, they talk all at once and all together, they break in even on themselves; on clang the clappers and leave no time for the excited metal to din itself out, for like a pendulum they are already back at the other edge, droning into its own droning.

a. How is rhythm used here to convey the impression being described more vividly?

* above the city

40

b. Comment on the way the author 'balances' his long, complex sentences.

c. This is the opening of a novel. What does it lead us to expect from the rest of the novel?

2. A marvellous stillness pervaded the world, and the stars, together with the serenity of their rays, seemed to shed upon the earth the assurance of everlasting security. The young moon, recurved, and shining low in the west, was like a slender shaving thrown up from a bar of gold, and the Arabian Sea, smooth and cool to the eye like a sheet of ice, extended its perfect level to the perfect circle of a dark horizon.

a. Comment on the movement of this passage, showing what it adds to the description.

3. I hasped the window; I combed his black long hair from his forehead; I tried to close his eyes: to extinguish, if possible, that frightful, life-like gaze of exultation before any one else beheld it. They would not shut: they seemed to sneer at my attempts: and his parted lips and sharp white teeth sneered too! Taken with another fit of cowardice, I cried out for Joseph. Joseph shuffled up and made a noise; but re-solutely refused to meddle with him.

a. The speaker is trying to 'dress' the corpse of a character who has stalked an entire novel with menace and violence. How do the rhythm and phrasing help to indicate the speaker's state of mind? (You should pay particular attention to the use of punctuation in this passage.)

CHAPTER 7

LANGUAGE
AND STYLE

In prose, as in poetry, *how* the thing is said is centrally important to *what* is being said. Indeed, whenever we use language — in letters, interviews, daily conversation — the tone we adopt (blunt, respectful, conciliatory, sarcastic) and the type of words we choose (academic, slang, jargon) are a vital part of the message we are trying to communicate — indicating, to a great extent, how we think, or feel, or how much we know, about what we are saying. George Orwell once observed that when we read anything worthwhile and well written we generally perceive a strong physical impression of what the writer would look, or sound like from the style of his writing.

This question of style highlights a major problem for the new student of A-Level English. It is all too easy to be impressed by a passage that resounds with flamboyant, or technical, or 'learned' language. On the other hand, an inexperienced reader may be contemptuous of a more accessible, direct and simple passage — because it is not 'literary' enough. Yet a 'high-flown' style frequently obscures the fact that the writer has little to say, or feels for his subject to any great depth, whereas a more unpretentious piece may speak with passion, urgency and power. This vague concept of 'literary' prose should be dispensed with early in the course.

ELEMENTS OF STYLE

1. Word selection

The first thing we will notice about any passage will be the type of words chosen. Within a passage there should be a consistency in the selection of language. Some of the more common 'types' of language the student will come across are:

Technical

The passage may centre on the use of terms specific to a given specialist area or discipline — such as the sciences, religion, philosophy, etc. Such language will be modified if the passage is intended for the layman, but may still be required to a certain extent if the subject is to be considered with any precision or depth. Technical language should never be employed merely for its own sake. It should add illumination and insight, as and when necessary. The student should consider whether or not he feels the writer has a sure grasp of his material and is genuinely at pains to express himself as lucidly as possible, or does he perhaps feel, as a reader, he is simply being bombarded with grandiose jargon from a writer who is more concerned with airing his own knowledge. The following is taken from J S Mill, where he begins to define what he means by his concept of 'Utilitarianism':

> Those who know anything about the matter are aware that
> every writer, from Epicurus to Bentham, who maintained the
> theory of utility, meant by it, not something contradistinguished
> from pleasure, but pleasure itself, together with exemption from
> pain; and instead of opposing the useful to the agreeable or
> ornamental, have always declared that the useful means these,
> among other things.

This is complex and abstract exposition, loaded with 'technical' terms from the discipline of Philosophy ("utility", "contradistinguished") and intimidating allusions ("Epicurus" and "Bentham"). Yet we sense the writer seeks clarity, simplifies (without becoming 'simplistic') where possible (as in the closing comments), and genuinely appears anxious to express and communicate the validity of his views (there is a certain urgency to the tone). Patient concentration allows the non-specialist to follow the line of argument without great difficulty.

Academic

Such language will be used to convey difficult or abstract concepts. The effect will be similar to that just outlined in 'technical' language. The student's main concern with such language is to ensure that he has the

43

necessary breadth of vocabulary to cope with such demanding writing. Analysis of such passages will be usefully given a sound context if the student considers the type of reader the passage is aimed at.

Prosaic

This may appear an odd term to use for the language of 'prose' (which is technically *all* prosaic in the original sense). I use it here to indicate a type of language at the opposite extreme of the previous two. The writer may deliberately adopt a homely, mundane, ordinary or flat style. Many modern novelists — especially American ones — have chosen just such a style — partly to create a vivid impression of human experiences as they are *actually* lived and partly as an artistic rebellion against the more elaborate, 'elitist' styles of previous ages. Here is the opening of a short story by John Updike:

> First, the boat trip home: a downpour in Liverpool, and on the
> wharf two girls (harlots?) singing 'Don't Sit Under the Apple
> Tree' under a single raincoat held over their heads like a canopy,
> everyone else huddling under the eaves of the warehouses, but
> these girls coming right down to the edge of the concrete wharf,
> singing, in effect to the whole ocean liner but more particularly
> to some person or persons (a pair of sailor lovers?) under the
> tourist deck.

The flat, mundane language here helps to convey the desired impression of an 'ordinary' person speaking simply and directly to the reader (posing questions almost as they occur to him in the flow of his recollections) and actually enhances the quality of seemingly routine descriptions, making them more vivid, realistic and memorable.

Colloquial

Such language will achieve an even greater degree of intimacy and 'immediacy' (i.e. give the reader a 'dramatic' sense of 'being there' with the writer) than the previous type of language. Generally, such writing will seek to lend pace, colour and a more vividly realistic sense of events and characters. Such writing is frequently used to indicate the 'character' of the narrator. Such effects are achieved in the following example from Hemingway:

> I guess looking at it, now, my old man was cut out for a fat
> guy, one of those regular little roly fat guys you see around, but
> he sure never got that way, except a little towards the last . . .

Such writing tends to produce an easy, comfortable rapport with the reader and details of such language are often unexpected, and vivid.

Dialect

This use of language is similar to the previous one, though here the writer will attempt to convey a precise impression of local setting or character. The writer seeks to create an authentic and realistic atmosphere. Many modern novelists have experimented with the possibilities of writing in dialect — although Scott and Hardy made valiant earlier efforts. There are real difficulties with dialect, both for the reader (use of unfamiliar, localized terms) and the writer (finding adequate — i.e. comprehensive, yet accurate — linguistic equivalents for such local pronunciations and speech rhythms) and these can disrupt the natural flow of the prose. However there is no doubting the vivid potential of dialect in prose, especially in the hands of a master such as Mark Twain.

Exotic, Foreign and Archaic Language

Such language is another device to give a passage a specific and vivid flavour. We have already seen an example of how Romantic prose can use exotic language to create a mysterious atmosphere. Many writers, such as Lawrence and Hemingway, achieve a vivid 'sense of place' by using 'local' terms when describing foreign locations. These are used mainly for atmospheric touches — a writer will not jeopardize 'losing' his reader with obscure or unexplained foreign words. The deliberate use of archaic language, old fashioned words and expressions, will also create a specific feeling. An entire passage may adopt the linguistic style of a previous age to achieve a certain effect. Lawrence, for example, frequently reverts to almost biblical language and speech rhythms to elevate important sections of *The Rainbow*.

Once again, the student should consider whether such effects of language actually contribute something vital to the passage, or whether they are merely contrived and 'clever'.

2. Dialogue

Dialogue, or direct speech, will make a passage of prose more dramatic, vivid and immediate. There is an art to writing dialogue effectively and many fine narrative and descriptive writers appear awkward and stilted when they attempt direct speech. When dialogue is employed, the student should consider the following questions:

a. Is it convincing? (i.e. does it sound like people actually speaking?)
b. What does it add to the 'characterization' of the speaker?
c. Are the 'speakers' clearly differentiated, or do they all sound like the author himself?
d. How is the dialogue arranged, in terms of its relationship to the rest of the writing?

Dialogue will also affect the rhythm of the prose, generally making it move far more quickly, especially such dramatic speech as argument and exclamation. Here is an example of effective, well-paced dialogue from Joseph Heller; the famous *Catch 22* is being patiently explained by the military doctor to a combat pilot desperate to avoid flying dangerous missions:

> Yossarian looked at him soberly and tried another approach. "Is Orr crazy?"
> "He sure is," Doc Daneeka said.
> "Can you ground him?"
> "I sure can. But first he has to ask me. That's part of the rule".
> "Then why doesn't he ask you to?"
> "Because he's crazy," Doc Daneeka said. "He has to be crazy to keep flying combat missions after all the close calls he's had. Sure, I can ground Orr. But first he has to ask me to".
> "That's all he has to do to be grounded?"
> "That's all. Let him ask me".
> "And then you can ground him?" Yossarian asked.
> "No. Then I can't ground him."
> "You mean there's a catch?"
> "Sure there's a catch," Doc Daneeka replied. "Catch 22. Anyone who wants to get out of combat duty isn't really crazy".
>
> *Catch 22*

3. Syntax and Phrasing

This will depend on the type of prose being written. Within the flow of narrative prose, syntax and phrasing should be unobtrusive, simply aiding the flow of events and descriptions at an appropriate pace. These elements, however, become more important in pieces concerned more with ideas rather than character, event or description. Here there will be a need for clarity in syntax and balance, pause and contrast in phrasing — as we have already seen in the prose of Milton, Dr Johnson and Macauley. The coherent flow of ideas must be maintained without 'overloading' sentence structure, to prevent crucial details being lost. Pauses must be introduced to allow major ideas to 'sink in'. There is a fine, short example of all this in Bacon's famous: "Reading maketh a full man; conference a ready man; and writing an exact man". Students should pay particular attention to the way a writer employs punctuation (especially the comma and the semi-colon) as it will control the pace of the writing. The modern trend may well be one that is moving towards a greater simplification of sentence and grammatical structure (indeed, the cultivation of a sophisticated style of syntax and phrasing, once so esteemed, now appears somewhat artificial and stilted), yet the modern writer is still aware of this need for balance and control when an important point is to be made, as in Lawrence's: "Be still when you have nothing to say; when genuine passion moves you, say what you've got to say, and say it hot".

Writers may occasionally invert normal word order for particular emphasis. Such 'licence' is more usually found in poetry, but can also be most effective in prose. We can see this in Dickens': "She was full of business, and undoubtedly was, as she told us, devoted to the cause"; Joyce's: "On all sides distorted reflections of her image started from his memory"; and Lincoln's famous: "Fourscore and seven years ago our fathers brought forth upon this continent a new nation".

4. Figurative Language, Metaphor, Imagery

All forms of language communication make frequent use of figurative language. ("He's a tough nut to crack", "the mouth of a river", "a thorny issue", "the foot of the stairs", "on top of the world" are all common examples of 'everyday' figurative language). Prose writers will frequently employ figurative devices — and for the same reason we all do — to make our expression more lively and vivid, more easy for our reader or listener to appreciate and comprehend in a full sense. A prose writer may even avail himself of the full range of poetic devices — such as imagery, metaphor, simile — even alliteration (Dickens' "bat in blisters, ball scorched brown"). Descriptive prose will depend heavily upon such devices for its atmospheric effect — and there is a fine example of this in our Reference Passage B (see page 49). Images may also be used to increase the emotional content of a passage, as in this example by F Scott Fitzgerald: "her mouth damp to his kisses and her eyes plaintive with melancholy and her freshness like new fine linen in the morning. Why, these things were no longer in the world!".

Characters in a narrative can be fixed forcefully in the mind's eye by a striking image, metaphor or simile. Charles Dickens is a master of just such effects ("If the conventional Cherub could ever grow up and be clothed, he might be photographed as a portrait of Wilfer", "Wegg was a knotty man . . . with a face carved out of very hard material . . . he was so wooden that he seemed to have taken his wooden leg naturally").

A contemplative, or philosophic passage may employ predominantly literal use of language, yet seal the main point or conclusion with an arresting piece of figurative expression. Other passages (such as "Time Passes", from *To the Lighthouse*) may seek to sustain a 'poetic intensity' throughout.

LANGUAGE, STYLE AND THE REFERENCE PASSAGES

Passage A

The language of the passage indicates two things here. Firstly, it has a slightly 'archaic' aspect ('refectory', 'eating house', 'grew to my imagination', 'scrivener'), and strongly suggests writing of the Victorian era. The second aspect relates more specifically to the character of the narrator, who is clearly an educated man ("pallid haughtiness", "tame compliance", "effectual succour") capable of perceptive insight (the observations on 'human sympathy').

The passage contains little figurative language, yet several phrases are effective and arresting, such as "quiet mysteries", "dead brick wall", "pallid haughtiness", "awed me into tame compliance" and — more emphatically — "common sense bids the soul be rid of it". In many ways, the most interesting aspect of style here lies in the syntactical structures. There is a high degree of order, organization and balance here, which again comments on the type of man the narrator himself is. The long second sentence of the first paragraph is precisely patterned through the use of comma and semi-colon. This basic, patterned repetition (*though such and such is the case, Bartleby never does the obvious or expected*) builds up most effectively to convey the exasperation the narrator feels in trying to comprehend Bartleby. To complement this, negatives abound — particularly that most emphatic of all negatives — 'never'.

As the narrator regains his 'composure' in the second paragraph, now resigned to the fact that Bartleby is beyond his assistance, syntax and phrasing become more controlled. We sense a more calm and balanced state of mind behind a sentence such as:

> As the forlornness of Bartleby grew and grew to my imagination, so did melancholy merge into fear, pity into repulsion.

This, we assume, is the turning-point in the narrator's attitude to Bartleby. There is a similar 'balance', this time tinged with finality and resignation, behind the final:

> I might give alms to his body, but it was his soul that suffered, and his soul I could not reach.

Passage B

This passage depends heavily on the use of detail for its effect and even the smallest of touches lends a subtle impact to the overall impression. The language itself is simple ("glued", "yapping", "squatting"), at times conversational ("There you had it all"), yet is fused with poetic richness. The opening "We" establishes the slightly unusual first person plural narrative that is more intimate and draws the reader (as part of the 'group') into the scene as well. Then the accumulation of atmospheric detail begins with "dusk", "high shallows", "points of Indian tents", "silhouettes" and "blanketed figures". The images conjured before the reader call on most of the senses. Visual images are strongly present — especially the feeling of "shadow" as light becomes dark. The two most striking visual images — the "white goats that flowed like water" and the lake, "pale in the dying light" capture this atmosphere perfectly as the last remnants of light. The mention of the 'car' strikes a deliberately alien and jarringly modern note over the primitive scene.

In the long, weaving sentence that closes the paragraph, the 'tapestry' is elaborately built up, piece by piece. There is a subtle use of repetition ("blanketed", "horsemen", "dusk", the "fires") that brings a sense of unity to the scene. The visual impression of the horsemen, "in big steeple hats sitting glued on their ponies", is particularly vivid. Aural impressions ("bells tinkling", "dogs yapping") and those of smell ("wood-smoke", "cooking") help to "fill out" the scene even more. The tableau seems totally static; figures "crouch", or "hover". Any movement seems slightly unreal, or extremely slow, as in the horsemen "crossing the dusk", or the "tilted wagons" (where again we notice a visual addition through the adjective) "trailing in on the trail below" (with its effective repetition). The adjectives and verbs continue to give more vivid touches of detail, in spite of their simplicity. The tents *prick* the ridge of the "vallum" (curiously, the only 'technical' term used, yet adding a certain exotic element); the alliterative "fires flickering in front" also "glitter"; women are "crouching bundles"; girls wear "full petticoats"; and the dogs are "thin-tailed".

There is a swaying rhythm to the "horsemen dipping down and emerging again" which, in itself, "acts out" the movement of the riders. Yet the most effective rhythmic element in this paragraph lies in the fading rhythm of the final "trail crossing the floor of the hollows in the low dusk" as the portrait is quietly completed.

There is a marked change at the opening of the second paragraph, as the writer speaks directly to the reader. The "hollow of your hand" recalls the "hollows" he has just described, and the homely simile preserves the simplicity of the passage. There is an effective balance to "born in England and kindled with Fenimore Cooper". The alliterative cliche of "wild and woolly West" is used deliberately to contrast with the 'reality' of the Red Indian he has just witnessed. There is a slight recall of the memorable atmosphere created in the first paragraph in the closing sentences. This first appears in the alliterative "nomad nations", who "gather still" (with, I feel, the dual association of 'still' — i.e. 'to this day' and 'silent', or 'unmoving') in the "continent of hemlock trees and prairies" — the only 'elevated' phrase in the entire passage. We are given closer detail of the Indians — now specifically named as Apaches — for the first time, with their "steeple black hats", "plaits wrapped with beaver fur", "silver beads" and "turquoise". Their speech is unexpected, "American or Spanish", as if to emphasize again the difference between our expectations of the Indians and the reality. The final impression — the "strange lines in their faces" — is a most effective means of recalling the mysteriousness of the earlier description.

Passage C

Stylistically, this represents the most varied of the three passages. Again, the language is not modern ("sallies", "youngling", "sage", etc.). It is also somewhat elevated and literary ("cloistered", "immortal garland", etc.). The basic means of presenting the abstract concepts of 'virtue' and 'vice' is through personification. Sheltered virtue that avoids all temptation is dealt with first. This is described by striking adjectives and balanced phrases — "fugitive and cloistered" and "unexercised and unbreathed". Its uselessness is conveyed through the metaphor of a race. Such virtue never "sallies out" into the race; instead it "slinks" away — an effective verb to suggest a timid surrendering of responsibility. The race for the "immortal garland" is life itself, which is vividly characterized by "heat and dust".

Other devices from poetry are in evidence in the passage. Normal word order is inverted in the phrase "Assuredly we bring not innocence into the world" to emphasize "not innocence" — the basic point being made. Personification continues in the following sentence, where virtue "is but a youngling" (a quaint phrase that deliberately draws attention to itself) and vice has "her" followers. Untried virtue is a "blank virtue" of "excremental whiteness" — a powerfully contemptuous dismissal. Alliteration emphasizes the esteem in which the writer holds the poet Spenser — "sage and serious poet Spenser". (The effect of alliteration, other than as an aural device, is to link the words together in the reader's mind; here Spenser is linked with sage and serious). There are other allusions to Scotus and Aquinas to indicate the learned quality of the writer's own mind. The allusion to a specific incident in Spenser's work is developed at some length in support of the writer's argument. The syntax and grammatical arrangement of this sentence is also typical of the passage as a whole. Such dense and weighty sentences require — and, in this passage, receive — care and sophistication in their structuring to keep the meaning clear. Commas and semi-colons are liberally employed to provide pause where necessary, without distorting the flow of the connecting ideas being expressed. In this sentence, the structure moves carefully to emphasize the short closing phrase — "and yet abstain".

In the final two sentences, the writer relinquishes such devices as personification to address the reader more directly. The penultimate sentence is another good example of the way the comma is used in this passage to control the flow of ideas without decreasing the momentum — especially here as the argument moves towards its conclusion. The language becomes more abstract and academic now — "so necessary to the constituting of human virtue" — although "the scanning of error to the confirmation of truth" is a richly resonant phrase and "scout" has a sharply vigilant edge. Through the confidence and assertiveness of the passage, the reader tends to feel he is being 'addressed' — as in a lecture. A traditional technique of such public speaking — the rhetorical question — is introduced here at the end of the sentence for added emphasis. We hear a strong and firm voice throughout this passage (even from the opening "I cannot praise . . .") and nowhere is this more in evidence than the phrasing of this question ("how can we more safely . . ."). The short final sentence — emphasized by its very brevity after such previously complex sentences — is a triumphant assertion that the argument has been conclusively proved. "And this . . ." immediately links with all that has just been said, while word order is once again inverted in the final phrase — "books promiscuously read" — to highlight the unexpected, and perhaps ironically appropriate "promiscuously".

Exercises

1.   "Gimme a chaw 'v tobacker, Hank".
     "Cain't; I hain't got but one chaw left. Ask Bill".
        Maybe Bill gives him a chaw, maybe he lies and says he ain't got

none. Some of them kind of loafers never has a cent in the world nor a chaw of tobacco of their own. They get all their chawing by borrowing; they say to a fellow, "I wish you'd len' me a chaw, Jack, I jist this minute give Ben Thompson the last chaw I had" — which is a lie pretty much every time, it don't fool nobody but a stranger, but Jack ain't no stranger, so he says:

"You give him a chaw, did you? So did your sister's cat's grandmother. You pay me back the chaws you've awready borry'd off'n me, Lafe Buckner, then I'll loan you one or two ton of it and won't charge you no back intrust, nuther".

a. Comment on the use of language in this passage by both the 'speakers' and the narrator.

b. Do you find such a passage effective, convincing or amusing? Give reasons for your comments.

2. Dombey was about eight-and-forty years of age. Son about eight-and-forty minutes. Dombey was rather bald, rather red, and though a handsome well-made man, too stern and pompous in appearance, to be prepossessing. Son was very bald, and very red, and though (of course) an undeniably fine infant, somewhat crushed and spotty in his general effect, as yet. On the brow of Dombey, Time and his brother Care had set some marks, as on a tree that was to come down in good time — remorseless twins they are for striding through their human forests, notching as they go — while the countenance of Son was crossed and recrossed with a thousand little creases, which the same deceitful Time would take delight in smoothing out and wearing away with the flat part of his scythe, as a preparation of the surface for his deeper operations.

a. Comment on the style of this passage.

b. The passage occurs at the opening of a famous novel, *Dombey and Son*. What are we led to expect about future events concerning the two main characters which are being introduced here?

3. The Smiths were unimpressed and drank the Coca-Cola with evident pleasure. "You will need something stronger than that where you are going", the purser said.

"My husband and I have never taken anything stronger", Mrs Smith replied.

"The water is not to be trusted, and you will find no Coca-Cola now that the Americans have moved out. At night when you hear the shooting in the streets you will think perhaps that a strong glass of rum . . ."

"Not rum", Mrs Smith said.

"Shooting?" Mr Smith inquired. "Is there shooting?" He looked at his wife where she sat crouched under the travelling-rug (she was not warm enough even in the stuffy cabin) with a trace of anxiety. "Why shooting?"

"Ask Mr Brown. He lives there".

I said, "I've not often heard shooting. They act more silently as a rule."

"Who are they?" Mr Smith asked.

"The Tontons Macoute", the purser broke in with wicked glee. "The President's bogey men. They wear dark glasses and they call on their victims after dark".

Mr Smith laid his hand on his wife's knee. "The gentleman is trying to scare us, my dear", he said. "They told us nothing about this at the tourist-bureau".

a. How is dialogue in this passage used to give an indication of the type of people the different speakers are?

b. How is dialogue used to develop humour and suspense?

c. Does such dialogue 'sound' realistic and effective?

4. The lower part of the castle was hollowed into several intricate cloisters; and it was not easy for one under so much anxiety to find the door that opened into the cavern. An awful silence reigned throughout those subterraneous regions, except now and then some blasts of wind that shook the doors she had passed, and which grating on the rusty hinges were re-echoed through that long labyrinth of darkness. Every murmur struck her with new terror; — yet more she dreaded to hear the wrathful voice of Manfred urging his domestics to pursue her. She trod as softly as her impatience would give her leave, — yet frequently stopped and listened to hear if she was followed. In one of those moments she thought she heard a sigh. She shuddered, and recoiled a few paces. In a moment she thought she heard the step of some person. Her blood curdled; she concluded it was Manfred. Every suggestion that horror could inspire rushed into her mind. She condemned her rash flight, which had thus exposed her to his rage in a place where her cries were not likely to draw any body to her assistance.

a. Comment on the use of detail in this passage as a means of developing suspense.

b. This passage comes from a 'Gothic' novel, tales of terror that were once immensely popular. Do you find the writer effective in conveying a sense of terror and suspense? Give reasons for your comments.

CHAPTER 8

INTENTION

The final part of any analysis should fully consider the 'intention' behind the writing of that passage. This is always best left to the end, as the student will by then have taken the longest possible time to familiarize himself with what is being said. Prose tends to be less elaborate and complex in its use of such constituent parts as imagery, etc. and concentrates more exclusively and clearly on 'meaning'.

When considering 'intention', the student will have to consider several questions. What is it that the author has really been trying to communicate? What is his motive? (i.e. to inform, persuade, entertain, describe, highlight, promote, etc.) It will be also worthwhile considering for whom the passage is intended (the general reader, the informed specialist, etc.). Final comments could suggest how far the writer's intention has been fulfilled as far as the student himself is concerned.

INTENTION AND THE REFERENCE PASSAGES

Passage A

This passage is most likely taken from a novel or short story. Its basic purpose is twofold. The first is to describe the mysterious personality of Bartleby and to show, with reference to specific, mundane details, how his behaviour differs from that of ordinary men. The second aim is to describe the narrator's attitude to that character and explain (and perhaps justify) how this reaction to Bartleby changes from one of pity and concern to one of frustration, fear and repulsion. The narrator is at some pains to show he does not lack sympathy, yet his inability to help, or even reach, Bartleby causes a hardening of attitude — a natural reaction the narrator feels, given such unyielding circumstances.

Passage B

This could also come from a novel, or story, or possibly an essay. Here the writer is concerned with giving as vivid an impression as possible of his first encounter with Apaches. The scene the writer came upon that dusk clearly made a deep impression on him and the wealth of detail he lavishes on his description is an attempt to allow the reader to share such feelings. He consequently seeks to involve as much of the reader's sensibility and senses as possible through an array of images. The passage is basically trying to communicate the *reality* of the life being lived now by the Apaches. Like most of us who have never actually *seen* such encampments, the writer approached the scene with preconceived ideas of the 'wild and woolly West'. It was the way in which the reality of the scene so differed from such misconceptions that most surprised the writer — and this dichotomy between reality and fiction (hence the reference to Cooper) is at the centre of the passage.

Passage C

Such a passage would most likely be found in an essay or treatise. Its specialist concern with moral philosophy is not intended for the general reader. The writer seeks to explain his philosophy as to what constitutes true virtue and develops this into an argument against censorship of books. The writer explains that "true" virtue must be able to confront and rise above vice, rather than simply hide from it, or avoid it. Such sheltered virtue is negative, worthless — an "excremental whiteness". Yet the tone and elaborate expression (through personification, etc.) suggest that the writer wishes to do more than simply inform the reader of his opinion. The confident and direct approach of the passage also suggest a didactic intention — that the writer wishes to persuade us to agree with him and think and act in the light of such opinions.

CHAPTER 9

WRITTEN
ANALYSIS AND
EXAMINATIONS

The points made concerning the written analysis in the previous book, 'Poetry Appreciation For A-Level', apply equally to poetry and prose. It is worth emphasizing that the syllabus stipulates that: "the intention of the questions is to test the candidate's ability to read literature critically"; that the student will be required to "organize his response to unseen passages"; and that the student should be able to "present that response as clearly and directly as possible". This highlights the basic process — a careful and sensitive *reading*, the *organization* of the ideas that arise from that reading, and the *presentation* of those ideas in a coherent written analysis.

As we have already indicated, it is vital that the initial part of the process — the reading — which, in terms of gaining marks, may appear the least important, be given due care and attention. Increasingly, examiners are specifying areas for comment (i.e. 'tone', 'movement', 'imagery', etc.) in prose analysis, so answers are more likely to organize *themselves* by following the prescribed guidelines. Random observations, commenced after a couple of quick readings, are unlikely to constitute an 'organized' response.

Examination rubric specifically requests students to "read carefully" and "refer directly" to the passage. Points made should always be supported by reference to, or quotation from, the passage itself. It is easier for the student to do this here than in the other papers in his English course. There, quotations have to be learnt. In prose and poetry appreciation the student should take full advantage of the fact that the text in question is in front of him, enabling him to quote relevantly and extensively. Lengthy quotations (i.e. those of more than two lines), however, should be avoided; here a general line, or section, reference will suffice.

If there are several questions on a passage, with no indication as to the allocation of marks per question, the student himself will have to decide which questions carry the bulk of the marks and arrange his time accordingly. A question asking for a 'brief outline of the situation, or events, or 'argument'' of a passage will not carry anything like the amount of marks accorded to a question which asks for an analysis of "the means by which the passage seeks to make its impact". The questions that direct the student towards detailed analysis of a passage's technique (i.e. use of 'tone', 'atmosphere', 'movement', 'imagery', etc.) will always carry the most marks.

PASSAGES FOR COMPARISON

When a question offers two passages for comparison, the basic process remains the same, with slight modifications as directed by the wording of the question. The passages will be 'linked' in some way that invites 'comparison' in the first place — usually, in prose, by their subject-matter (i.e. two descriptions of a house, or a person; two passages concerning death, or birth, or marriage — and so on). The analysis will be concerned with establishing what it is the passages have in common, then looking at the *differences* in the two treatments of a similar theme. Again, the question is likely to outline certain areas for comment. The student may approach the question by taking the two passages separately, dealing with the first in its entirety, followed by the second — where constant references of comparison and contrast can be made back to the first passage; or, the student may approach the question under the headings of the elements designated for comment — i.e. looking at the use the two passages make of 'tone', then going on to 'movement', etc. Either approach is acceptable and the student may choose after his own preference.

SAMPLE ANALYSIS

The following is intended as a 'sample' of prose appreciation 'in action'. It is not intended as a 'model answer'. It is simply designed to indicate the way prose analysis can be approached and arranged and to display the sort of depth and detail a student could reasonably be expected to go into in the time allowed. It will not say everything that could be said about the passage, but, as a structured, working example, it should give the student a firm idea of the type and range of comment that an examiner would expect from a full answer.

The passage and instructions are taken from a previous A-Level paper.

Read carefully the passage printed below. Say how convincing a presentation of war the passage gives you. You should support your answer by close reference to the text.

The weather was mostly clear and cold; sometimes sunny at midday, but always cold. Here and there in the soil of the hillsides you found the green beaks of wild crocuses or irises poking through; evidently spring was coming, but coming very slowly. The nights were colder than ever. Coming off guard in the small hours we used to rake together what was left of the cook-house fire and then stand in the red-hot embers. It was bad for your boots, but it was very good for your feet. But there were mornings when the sight of dawn among the mountain-tops made it almost worthwhile to be out of bed at godless hours. I hate mountains, even from a spectacular point of view. But sometimes the dawn breaking behind the hill-tops in our rear, the first narrow streaks of gold, like swords slitting the darkness, and then growing light and the seas of carmine cloud stretching away into inconceivable distances, were worth watching even when you had been up all night, when your legs were numb from the knees down, and you were sullenly reflecting that there was no hope of food for another three hours. I saw the dawn oftener during this campaign than during the rest of my life put together — or during the part that is to come, I hope.

We were short-handed here, which meant longer guards and more fatigues. I was beginning to suffer a little from lack of sleep which is inevitable even in the quietest kind of war. Apart from guard-duties and patrols there were constant night-alarms and stand-to's, and in any case you can't sleep properly in a beastly hole in the ground with your feet aching with the cold. In my first three or four months in the line I do not suppose I had more than a dozen periods of twenty-four hours that were completely without sleep; on the other hand I certainly did not have a dozen nights of full sleep. Twenty or thirty hours' sleep in a week was quite a normal amount. The effects of this were not quite so bad as might be expected; one grew very stupid, and the job of climbing up and down the hills grew harder instead of easier, but one felt well and one was constantly hungry — heavens, how hungry! All food seemed good, even the eternal haricot beans which everyone in Spain finally learned to hate the sight of. Our water, what there was of it, came from miles away, on the backs of mules or little persecuted donkeys. For some reason the Aragon peasants treated their mules well but their donkeys abominably. If a donkey refused to go it was quite usual to kick him in the testicles. The issue of candles had ceased, and matches were running short. The Spaniards taught us how to make olive oil lamps out of a condensed milk tin, a cartridge-clip, and a bit of rag. When you had any olive oil, which was not often, these things would burn with a smoky flicker, about a quarter of candle power, just enough to find your rifle by.

Analysis

This piece of descriptive prose provides a first-hand account of the ordinary soldiers' experiences during war — presumably the Spanish Civil War, from references in the text and the modern language. The passage is written in effectively simple language that is generally conversational ("in the soil of the hill-sides you found . . .") and colloquial ("short-handed", "can't", "beastly hole"). Indeed there is a strong impression conveyed of an actual soldier — with his references to "stand-to's", "fatigues", etc. — talking directly to the reader in a personal, almost casual manner.

Impressions of the type of life such soldiers led are conveyed by various means. There is a dull, lifeless tone behind most of the descriptions. The atmosphere is "cold", dreary, colourless and wintery. The passage moves with a weary, lugubrious monotony. This all helps create a predominant mood that is only broken once — when the writer talks of the break of dawn.

The passage relies mainly on its use of telling detail to make its impression. This is especially so in the first paragraph, which deals with the soldiers' immediate environment. There is a precise balance to the opening sentence, where the alliterative "clear and cold" are particularly highlighted. There is also balance to the second sentence — again through the use of the semi-colon — yet here the weary rhythm is established, especially in the final phrase "but coming very slowly". The green "beaks" of the flowers, "poking" through, have a harsh quality of struggle about them. The description of the soldiers standing in the red-hot embers is one of the many precise details the writer introduces to make his account more vivid and realistic. The neatly balanced and effective sentence: It was bad for your boots, but it was very good for your feet — where complete 'balance' is only prevented by the significant addition of "very" — introduces a note of sardonic, ironic humour that will appear even more effectively at the end.

This is followed by the description of the dawn. Tone and atmosphere are changed by the use of "But" as the mountains at dawn "almost" (an important qualifier) make it worth being awake at such "godless hours". We are reminded of the personal, subjective nature of the account when the writer informs us: "I hate mountains". This description of the beauties

59

of nature, emphasized by the contrasting ugliness of the surrounding war, produces a more elevated and heightened style of writing. Poetic similes — "like swords slitting the darkness" (an effectively violent image that keeps the feeling of war in the reader's mind, as it undoubtedly was constantly in the soldier's) — and images — "first narrow streaks of gold", "seas of carmine cloud stretching away into inconceivable distances" — are presented in delicately arranged phrases. There is, perhaps, a slightly self-conscious, contrived and overly poetic quality here — especially in the alliterated "carmine cloud" — and the passage tends to work more effectively at its simpler stylistic level. The rhythm of this sentence conveys an effective sense of the weary soldier trudging back to camp and being arrested by such a sight. Again we are reminded of the presence of war in the somewhat menacing manner in which the paragraph closes ("or during the part that is to come, I hope").

The second paragraph is concerned more with the type of life the soldier led in this situation. There is a further ominous quality to lack of sleep being "inevitable even in the quietest kind of war" — the implication being that this war is not 'quiet'. Again, semi-technical terms ("guard-duties", "night-alarms", "stand-to's") enhance the realism of the passage. The effectively colloquial "beastly hole" conveys the soldier's sense of annoyance and frustration, further emphasized by the hard sounds of "aching with cold". There is a resignation behind the way the writer elaborates the specific details, in terms of hours, of the lack of sleep — yet it is not a bitter, or gloomy resignation ("quite a normal amount", "The effects of this were not so bad as might be expected"). The results of too little sleep — "one grew very stupid, etc . . ." (where 'stupid' is a surprising, yet powerful evocation of the deadened weariness) — are outlined in a heavy, pronounced rhythm. Yet this is lightened finally by "but one felt well". The reader becomes attracted by the writer's simple, yet stoic, tolerance and lack of self-pity and real complaint, although the problem of hunger is given extra emphasis by the conversational exclamation — "heavens, how hungry!"

The passage then closes on a series of details that lend a more specific sense of place. Up to this point, the passage could have taken place almost anywhere, but now we find several touches of vivid, realistic 'local colour'. This comes in the type of food ("everyone in Spain" comes to "hate the sight" of the "eternal haricot beans"), the way the Aragon peasants treat the "persecuted" donkeys (where their violent abuse of the animals — "it was quite usual to kick him in the testicles" — is yet another subtle reminder of the violence of the war) and the home-made olive oil lamps. These details again help to convey the general scene to the reader, enabling him to imagine the soldiers' experiences more clearly. The final note, however, appropriately returns us to the dominant theme. The oil lamps, it seems only give enough light "to find your rifle by". This grimly, ironic final touch serves as an impressive reminder of the harshness and danger and frustration of the writer's situation and the stoic, almost good-natured manner in which he accepts it.

This passage seeks to give a vivid, personal account of the writer's experience of war. It is concerned solely with presenting the reality of that situation and refrains from any comment on war in general, or even the writer's own emotions and deeper feelings. It succeeds through the simplicity of its style and the directness of its approach. The impressions remain memorable through a perceptive use of detail. The writer deals with an experience which few contemporary readers will have undergone, yet which, 'imaginatively', he has enabled us to share.

Exercises

The previous pages have dealt with the specific areas of prose analysis that differ in emphasis from poetry analysis. Yet, in many ways, the most important part of the course on prose appreciation lies in actual practice. The following exercises are designed to meet this need. The exercises begin by offering questions that will direct the student to the more significant aspects of the given passages. These 'aids' will diminish as the exercises progress and the student's awareness of the intricacies of prose analysis increases. The final passages, which will include questions from past Advanced Level papers, will leave the student full-length analyses without assistance.

These exercises may be undertaken as written assignments or used as a basis for general discussion. The questions are only intended to guide the student. As such, they may profitably be 'ignored' in open discussion, or replaced with questions more appropriate to a particular class.

1. The dream was gone. Something had been taken from him. In a sort of panic he pushed the palms of his hands into his eyes and tried to bring up a picture of the waters lapping on Sherry Island and the moonlit veranda, and gingham on the golf links and the dry sun and the gold colour of her neck's soft down. And her mouth damp to his kisses and her eyes plaintive with melancholy and her freshness like new fine linen in the morning. Why, these things were no longer in the world! They had existed and they existed no longer.

   For the first time in years the tears were streaming down his face. But they were for himself now. He did not care about mouth and eyes and moving hands. He wanted to care, and he could not care. For he had gone away and he could never go back anymore. The gates were closed, the sun was gone down, and there was no beauty but the grey beauty of steel that withstands all time. Even the grief he could have borne was left behind in the country of illusion, of youth, of the richness of life, where his winter dreams had flourished.

"Long ago", he said, "long ago, there was something in me, but now that thing is gone. Now that thing is gone, that thing is gone. I cannot cry. I cannot care. That thing will come back no more".

a. This passage falls at the end of a short story. What do you imagine to be the character's situation here?
b. What is the character's state of mind in this extract? How does the author attempt to give the reader an impression of this?
c. How would you describe the tone of the passage?
d. Comment on the rhythm of the first paragraph.
e. What sort of life is suggested on 'Sherry Island'?
f. What is the effect of introducing direct speech in the final paragraph?
g. Do you find the passage effectively written?

2. There's more *to* a bluejay than any other creature. He has got more moods, and more different kinds of feelings than other creatures; and mind you, whatever a bluejay feels, he can put into language. And no mere commonplace language, either, but rattling, out-and-out book talk — and bristling with metaphor, too — just bristling! And as for command of language — why *you* never see a bluejay stuck for a word. No man ever did. They just boil out of him! And another thing I've noticed a good deal, there's no bird, or cow, or anything that uses as good grammar as a bluejay. You may say a cat uses good grammar. Well, a cat does — but you let a cat get excited once; you let a cat get to pulling fur with another cat on a shed, nights, and you'll hear grammar that will give you the lockjaw. Ignorant people think its the *noise* which fighting cats make that is so aggravating, but it ain't so; it's the sickening grammar they use. Now I've never heard a jay use bad grammar but seldom; and when they do, they are as ashamed as a human; they shut right down and leave.

a. How would you describe the tone of this passage? What sort of person do you imagine the narrator to be?
b. What 'type' of language does the writer use here?
c. What is the writer trying to achieve in a passage like this?
d. Do you find the passage effective?

3. Now, I saw in my dream, that by this time Pliable was got home to his house again, so that his neighbours came to visit him; and some of them called him a wise man for coming back, and some called him a

fool for hazarding himself with Christian: others, again, did mock at his cowardliness; saying, Surely, since you began to venture, I would not have been so base to have given out for a few difficulties. So Pliable sat sneaking among them. But at last he got more confidence, and then they all turned their tales, and began to deride poor Christian behind his back. And thus much concerning Pliable.

Now, as Christian was walking solitarily by himself, he espied one afar off, come crossing over the field to meet him; and their hap was to meet just as they were crossing the way of each other. The gentleman's name was Mr Worldly Wiseman: he dwelt in the town of Carnal Policy, a very great town, and also hard-by from whence Christian came. This man, then, meeting with Christian, and having some inkling of him, — for Christian's setting forth from the City of Destruction was much noised abroad, not only in the town where he dwelt, but also it began to be the town talk in some other places, — Mr Worldly Wiseman, therefore, having some guess of him, by beholding his laborious going, by observing his sighs and groans, and the like, began thus to enter into some talk with Christian.

a. Outline the events described in this extract.
b. Comment on the style of writing.
c. Comment on the use of names in this passage.
d. Such writing, where characters 'represent' abstract concepts, is called allegorical. Why should a writer choose to write in such a way, rather than, say, writing a straightforward essay about his opinions and beliefs?
e. Do you find such writing effective? Give reasons either way.

4. "Get into bed again, do! There's a dear! You're shivering".
White Sophia obeyed. It was true; she was shivering. Constance awoke. Mrs Baines went to the dressing-table and filled the egg-cup out of the bottle.
"Who's that for, Mother?" Constance asked sleepily.
"It's for Sophia", said Mrs Baines with good cheer. "Now, Sophia!" and she advanced with the egg-cup in one hand and the table-spoon in the other.
"What is it, Mother?" asked Sophia, who well knew what it was.
"Castor-oil, my dear", said Mrs Baines, winningly.
The ludicrousness of attempting to cure obstinacy and yearnings for a freer life by means of castor-oil is perhaps less real than apparent. The strange interdependence of spirit and body, though only understood intelligently in these intelligent days, was guessed at by sensible mediaeval mothers. And certainly, at the period when Mrs Baines

represented modernity, castor-oil was still the remedy of remedies. It had supplanted cupping*. And, if part of its vogue was due to its extreme unpleasantness, it had at least proved its qualities in many a contest with disease. Less than two years previously old Dr Harrop, being then aged eighty-six, had fallen from top to bottom of his stair-case. He had scrambled up, taken a dose of castor-oil at once, and on the morrow was as well as if he had never seen a staircase. This episode was town property and had sunk deep into all parts.

a. What is the situation in this extract?
b. What impression do you form of the characters involved? What means of 'characterization' does the writer employ?
c. How would you describe the tone of the final paragraph?
d. By what means does the writer introduce an element of humour into the passage?
e. What do you understand the last sentence to mean?
f. Does such writing appeal to you?

5. Silently the men approached the Great Ponds. The smell of fresh water and decaying vegetation filled their nostrils. It was a pleasant smell reminiscent of many highly rewarding fishing sessions. They brought out long bamboo poles from where they had been secreted and with them shoved off on the rafts. It was impossible to avoid the liquid sound of the poles as they pushed along, but fortunately the sound was indistinguishable from that made by the many fish drinking and surfacing playfully in the ponds.

During the rainy season the Great Ponds formed one mysterious stagnant sea of reddish-brown water ranging in depth from the waist to four or more times the height of a man. Fishing was not done then. Only the palm-wine tappers disturbed the chilly placidity of the dark waters with their rafts heavily loaded with calabashes of white effer-vescent palm wine begging to be drunk. The wine-tapping was easy since a man standing on his raft needed no ladder to reach the top of the palm wine tree.

During the dry season the floods subsided. What water was left collected in individual ponds restless with fish. At this stage the ponds were not completely isolated, but linked to one another by narrow necks of water barely navigable with rafts.

Villagers did not wait until the middle of the dry season. Fishing usually started towards the end of the rainy season when thundery showers often bathed the sweating bodies of eager fishermen.

* blood-letting

a. What type of prose is this?
b. Comment on the atmosphere. Choose specific details that best convey the atmosphere.
c. Comment on the language of the passage.
d. The passage is concerned with a scene in remote Africa — the sort of scene few readers have actually experienced. Does the passage vividly evoke a 'spirit of place' for you — i.e. does it create a strong impression of what the place is really like in your imagination?

6. The main facts in human life are five: birth, food, sleep, love and death. One could increase the number — add breathing for instance — but these five are the most obvious. Let us briefly ask ourselves what part they play in our lives, and what in novels. Does the novelist tend to reproduce them accurately or does he tend to exaggerate, minimize, ignore, and to exhibit his characters going through processes which are not the same through which you and I go, though they bear the same names?

To consider the two strangest first: birth and death; strangest because they are at the same time experiences and not experiences. We only know of them by report. We were all born, but we cannot remember what it was like. And death is coming even as birth has come, but, similarly, we do not know what it is like. Our final experience, like our first, is conjectural. We move between two darknesses. Certain people pretend to tell us what birth and death are like: a mother, for instance, has her point of view about birth, a doctor, a religious, have their points of view about both. But it is all from the outside, and the two entities who might enlighten us, the baby and the corpse, cannot do so, because their apparatus for communicating their experiences is not attuned to our apparatus for reception.

a. How would you briefly summarize the writer's 'subject-matter' here?
b. How would you describe this type of prose and where would you expect to find such a passage?
c. Why are birth and death, in the author's terms, the 'strangest' of · human experiences?
d. Do you agree with the writer's basic argument? Is it effectively stated?

7. True! — nervous — very, very dreadfully nervous I had been and am; but why *will* you say that I am mad? The disease had sharpened my senses — not destroyed — not dulled them. Above all was the sense of hearing acute. I heard all things in the heaven and in the earth. I heard many things in hell. How, then, am I mad? Hearken! and observe how healthily — how calmly I can tell you the whole story.

It is impossible to say how first the idea entered my brain; but once conceived, it haunted me day and night. Object there was none. Passion there was none. I loved the old man. He had never wronged me. He had never given me insult. For his gold I had no desire. I think it was his eye! Yes, it was this! One of his eyes resembled that of a vulture — a pale blue eye, with a film over it. Whenever it fell upon me, my blood ran cold; and so by degrees — very gradually — I made up my mind to take the life of the old man, and thus rid myself of the eye forever.

a. Comment on how rhythm is used in this passage to convey the speaker's state of mind.
b. Comment on the language of this passage.
c. How would you describe the tone of the speaker?
d. Do you feel, in spite of the speaker's protestations, that he is, in fact, mad? If so, do you find the passage a successful attempt to portray the insane mind?

8. Before the house-maid had lit their fire the next day, or the sun gained any power over a cold, gloomy morning in January, Marianne, only half dressed, was kneeling against one of the window-seats for the sake of all the little light she could command from it, and writing as fast as a continual flow of tears would permit her. In this situation, Elinor, roused from sleep by her agitation and sobs, first perceived her; and after observing her for a few moments with silent anxiety, said, in a tone of the most considerate gentleness.

"Marianne, may I ask?" —

"No, Elinor," she replied, "ask nothing; you will soon know all".

The sort of desperate calmness with which this was said lasted no longer than while she spoke, and was immediately followed by a return of the same excessive affliction. It was some minutes before she could go on with her letter, and the frequent bursts of grief which still obliged her, at intervals, to withhold her pen, were proofs enough of her feeling how more than probable it was that she was writing for the last time to Willoughby.

a. What do you imagine to be the situation behind this extract?
b. Comment on the way in which the writer handles Marianne's emotional state.
c. Comment on the effect of the direct speech.
d. Is the passage written in such a way to arouse your interest to wish to read the novel further?

9. Being in the hospital was better than being over Bologna or flying over

Avignon with Huple and Dobbs at the controls and Snowden dying in back.

There were usually not nearly as many sick people inside the hospital as Yossarian saw outside the hospital, and there were generally fewer people inside the hospital who were seriously sick. There was a much lower death rate inside the hospital than outside the hospital, and a much healthier death rate. Few people died unnecessarily. People knew a lot more about dying inside the hospital and made a much neater, more orderly job of it. They couldn't dominate Death inside the hospital, but they certainly made her behave. They had taught her manners. They couldn't keep Death out, but while she was in she had to act like a lady. People gave up the ghost with delicacy and taste inside the hospital. There was none of that crude, ugly ostentation about dying that was so common outside the hospital. They did not blow up in mid-air like Kraft or the dead man in Yossarian's tent, or freeze to death in the blazing summertime the way Snowden had frozen to death after spilling his secret to Yossarian in the back of the plane.

a. This passage concerns a fighter pilot who 'escapes' the perils of war by claiming to be sick and being placed in hospital. In what way is the passage above a 'satire' against war? You should pay special attention to the tone and use of humour.

b. The humour of this passage concerns serious, 'non-humorous' matters and is usually called 'black' humour. Is it effective here?

c. How serious do you feel is the writer's basic intention?

10. Under the eaves of a bicycle shop across the High Street an oyster stall was yellowly, smokily lit by a flambeau with a thick spongy wick. Oysters lay in a shining heap, many-faceted, grey and black and yellow. Two bottles, stopped with twists of brown paper, contained red peppersauce.

Postponing the salmon, Mr Biswas crossed the road and asked the man, "How the oysters going?"

"Two for a cent".

"Start opening".

The man shouted, released into happy activity. From somewhere in the darkness a woman came running up. "Come on", said the man. "Help open them". They put a bucket of water on the stall, washed the oysters, opened them with short blunt knives, and washed them again. Mr Biswas poured peppersauce into the shell, swallowed, held out his hand for another. The peppersauce scalded his lips.

The oyster man was talking drunkenly, in a mixture of Hindi and

English. "My son is a helluva man. I feel that something is seriously wrong with him. One day he put a tin can on the fence and come running inside the house. "The gun, Pa," he said. "Quick, give me the gun". I give him the gun. He run to the window and shoot. The tin can fall. "Pa," he say. "Look. I shoot work. I shoot ambition. They dead." The flambeau dramatized the oyster man's features, filling hollows with shadow, putting a shine on his temples, above his eyebrows, along his nose, along his cheek-bones. Suddenly he flung down his knife and pulled out a stick from below his stall. He waved the stick in front of Mr Biswas. "Anybody!" he said. "Tell anybody to come!"

a.   Comment on the style, language and movement of this passage.

11. Taking up the subject, then, upon general grounds, I ask what is meant by the word Poet? What is a Poet? To whom does he address himself? And what language is to be expected from him? He is a man speaking to men: a man, it is true, endued with a more lively sensibility, more enthusiasm and tenderness, who has a greater knowledge of human nature, and a more comprehensive soul, than are supposed to be common among mankind; a man pleased with his own passions and volitions, and who rejoices more than other men in the spirit of life that is in him; delighting to contemplate similar volitions and passions as manifested in the goings-on of the Universe, and habitually impelled to create them where he does not find them. To these qualities he has added a disposition to be more affected than other men by absent things as if they were present; an ability of conjuring up in himself passions, which are indeed far from being the same as those produced by real events, yet (especially in those parts of the general sympathy which are pleasing and delightful) do more nearly resemble the passions produced by real events, than any thing which, from the motions of their own minds merely, other men are accustomed to feel in themselves; whence, and from practice, he has acquired a greater readiness and power in expressing what he thinks and feels, and especially those thoughts and feelings which, by his own choice, or from the structure of his own mind, arise in him without immediate external excitement.

a.   Summarize the characteristics of a 'poet' outlined by the writer here.
b.   Comment on the phrasing and movement of this passage.
c.   Comment on the language used here.
d.   With which aspects of the author's definition of a 'poet' do you agree, or disagree?

12. The high grey-flannel fog of winter closed off the Salinas Valley from the sky and from all the rest of the world. On every side it sat like a lid on the mountains and made of the great valley a closed pot. On the broad, level land floor the gangplows bit deep and left the black earth shining like metal where the shares had cut. On the foothill ranches across the Salinas River, the yellow stubble fields seemed to be bathed in pale cold sunshine, but there was no sunshine in the valley now in December. The thick willow scrub along the river flamed with sharp and positive yellow leaves.

It was a time of quiet and of waiting. The air was cold and tender. A light wind blew up from the southwest so that the farmers were mildly hopeful of a good rain before long; but fog and rain do not go together.

Across the river, on Henry Allen's foothill ranch there was little work to be done, for the hay was cut and stored and the orchards were plowed up to receive the rain deeply when it should come. The cattle on the higher slopes were becoming shaggy and rough-coated.

a. Write a critical appreciation of this passage. You should pay particular attention to tone, atmosphere, movement and use of language.

13. As we determined when we first sat down to write this history, to flatter no man, but to guide our pen throughout by the directions of truth, we are obliged to bring our hero on the stage in a much more disadvantageous manner than we could wish; and to declare honestly, even at his first appearance, that it was the universal opinion of all Mr Allworthy's family, that he was certainly born to be hanged.

Indeed, I am sorry to say, there was too much reason for this conjecture. The lad having, from his earliest years, discovered a propensity to many vices, and especially to one, which hath as direct a tendency as any other to that fate, which we have just now observed to have been prophetically denounced against him. He had been already convicted of three robberies, viz. of robbing an orchard, of stealing a duck out of a farmer's yard, and of picking Master Blifil's pocket of a ball.

The vices of this young man were, moreover, heightened, by the disadvantageous light in which they appeared, when opposed to the virtues of Master Blifil, his companion: a youth of so different a cast from little Jones, that not only the family, but the all the neighbour-hood, resounded his praises. He was, indeed, a lad of remarkable disposition; sober, discreet, and pious, beyond his age. Qualities which gained him the love of everyone who knew him, whilst Tom Jones was universally disliked; and many expressed their wonder, that

Mr Allworthy would suffer such a lad to be educated with his nephew, lest the morals of the latter should be corrupted by his example.

a. Analyse the writer's method of narrative here.
b. Comment on the characterization of Tom Jones in this passage, paying special attention to tone, language and movement.

14. Cecil entered.

Appearing thus late in the story, Cecil must be at once described. He was medieval. Like a Gothic statue. Tall and refined, with shoulders that seemed braced square by an effort of the will, and a head that was tilted a little higher than the usual level of vision, he resembled those fastidious saints who guard the portals of a French cathedral. Well educated, well endowed, and not deficient physically, he remained in the grip of a certain devil whom the modern world knows as self-consciousness, and whom the medieval, with dimmer vision, worshipped as asceticism. A Gothic statue implies celibacy, just as a Greek statue implies fruition, and perhaps this is what Mr Beebe meant. And Freddy, who ignored history and art, perhaps meant the same when he failed to imagine Cecil wearing another fellow's cap.

a. Compare this passage with the previous one in terms of tone, attitude to the reader, technique of characterization and use of language.

15. "There will be a real time of it," muttered the bee-hunter, laughing, "if the boys get at work, in good earnest, with these red skins!"

He was interrupted by a general movement which took place among the band. The Indians dismounted to a man, giving their horses in charge to three or four of the party, who were also entrusted with the safe keeping of the prisoners. They then formed themselves in a circle round a warrior, who appeared to possess the chief authority; and at a given signal the whole array moved slowly and cautiously from the centre in straight and consequently diverging lines. Most of their dark forms blended with the brown covering of the prairie; though the captives, who watched the slightest movement of their enemies with vigilant eyes, were now and then enabled to discern a human figure, drawn against the horizon, as some one, more eager than the rest, rose to his greatest height in order to extend the limits of his view. But it was not long before even these fugitive glimpses of the moving, and constantly increasing circle, were lost, and uncertainty and conjecture were added to apprehension. In this manner passed many anxious and weary minutes, during the close of which the listeners expected at each moment to hear the whoop of the assailants and the shrieks of the assailed, rising together on the stillness of the night. But it would seem, that the search which was so evidently making, was without a sufficient object; for at the expiration of half an hour the different individuals of the band began to return singly, gloomy and sullen, like men who were disappointed.

"Our time is at hand," observed the trapper, who noted the smallest incident, or the slightest indication of hostility among the savages; "we are now to be questioned; and if I know anything of the policy of our case, I should say it would be wise to choose one among us to hold the discourse, in order that our testimony may agree. And furthermore, if an opinion from one as old and as worthless as a hunter of fourscore, is to be regarded, I would just venture to say, that man should be the one most skilled in the natur' of an Indian, and that he should also know something of their language — Are you acquainted with the tongue of the Siouxes, friend?"

a. Write a critical appraisal of this passage.
b. The passage is taken from the writer, Fenimore Cooper, quoted in Reference Passage B. Compare the two passages in terms of the writer's attitudes to the Indians and the different impressions conveyed to the reader.

16. Norcombe Hill — not far from Toller-Down — was one of the spots which suggests to a passer-by that he is in the presence of a shape approaching the indestructible as nearly any to be found on earth. It was a featureless convexity of chalk and soil — an ordinary specimen of those smoothly-outlined protuberances of the globe which may remain undisturbed on some great day of confusion, when far grander heights and dizzy granite precipices topple down.

The hill was covered on its northern side by an ancient and decaying plantation of beeches, whose upper verge formed a line over the crest, fringing its arched curve against the sky, like a mane. To-night these trees sheltered the southern slope from the keenest blasts, which smote the wood and floundered through it with a sound as of grumbling, or gushed over its crowning boughs in a weakened moan. The dry leaves in the ditch simmered and boiled in the same breezes, a tongue of air occasionally ferreting out a few, and sending them spinning across the grass. A group or two of the latest in date amongst the dead multitude had remained till this very mid-winter time on the twigs which bore them, and in falling rattled against the trunks with smart raps.

Between this half-wooded, half-naked hill, and the vague, still horizon that its summit indistinctly commanded, was a mysterious sheet of fathomless shade — the sounds from which suggested that what it concealed bore some reduced semblance to features here. The thin grasses, more or less coating the hill, were touched by the wind in breezes of differing powers, and almost of differing natures — one rubbing the blades heavily, another raking them piercingly, another brushing them like a soft broom. The instinctive act of humankind was to stand and listen, and learn how the trees on the right and the trees on the left wailed or chanted to each other in the regular antiphonies of a cathedral choir; how hedges and other shapes to leeward then caught the note, lowering it to the tenderest sob; and how the hurrying gust then plunged into the south, to be heard no more.

a. Write a critical appraisal of this passage, paying special attention to atmosphere, language, movement and use of imagery.

The following questions and instructions are all taken from previous Advanced Level examination papers.

17. The following passage is the opening of a short story. Say how well you think the author has succeeded in capturing the attention and interest of the reader, basing your answer on a close examination of the text.

It was nearly bed-time and when they awoke next morning land would be in sight. Dr Macphail lit his pipe and, leaning over the rail, searched the heavens for the Southern Cross. After two years at the front and a wound that had taken longer to heal than it should, he was glad to settle down quietly at Apia for twelve months at least, and he felt already better for the journey. Since some of the passengers were leaving the ship next day at Pago-Pago they had had a little dance that evening and in his ears hammered still the harsh notes of the mechanical piano. But the deck was quiet at last. A little way off he saw his wife in a long chair talking with the Davidsons, and he strolled over to her. When he sat down under the light and took off his hat you saw that he had very red hair, with a bald patch on the crown, and the red, freckled skin which accompanies red hair; he was a man of forty, thin, with a pinched face, precise and rather pedantic; and he spoke with a Scots accent in a very low, quiet voice.

Between the Macphails and the Davidsons, who were missionaries, there had arisen the intimacy of shipboard which is due to propinquity rather than to any community of taste. Their chief tie was the disapproval they shared of the men who spent their days and nights in the smoking-room playing poker or bridge and drinking. Mrs Macphail was not a little flattered to think that she and her husband were the only people on board with whom the Davidsons were willing to associate, and even the doctor, shy but no fool, half unconsciously acknowledged the compliment. It was only because he was of an argumentative mind that in their cabin at night he permitted himself to carp.

'Mrs Davidson was saying she didn't know how they'd have got through the journey if it hadn't been for us,' said Mrs Macphail, as she neatly brushed out her transformation. 'She said we were really the only people on the ship they cared to know.'

'I shouldn't have thought a missionary was such a big bug that he could afford to put on frills.'

'It's not frills. I quite understand what she means. It wouldn't have been very nice for the Davidsons to have to mix with all that rough lot in the smoking-room.'

'The founder of their religion wasn't so exclusive,' said Dr Macphail with a chuckle.

'I've asked you over and over again not to joke about religion,' answered his wife. 'I shouldn't like to have a nature like yours, Alec. You never look for the best in people.'

He gave her a sidelong glance with his pale, blue eyes, but did not reply. After many years of married life he had learned that it was more conducive to peace to leave his wife with the last word. He was undressed before she was, and climbing into the upper bunk he settled down to read himself to sleep.

When he came on deck next morning they were close to land. He looked at it with greedy eyes. There was a thin strip of silver beach rising quickly to hills covered to the top with luxuriant vegetation. The coconut trees, thick and green, came nearly to the water's edge, and among them you saw the grass houses of the Samoans; and here and there, gleaming white, a little church. Mrs Davidson came and stood beside him. She was dressed in black and wore round her neck a gold chain, from which dangled a small cross. She was a little woman, with brown, dull hair very elaborately arranged, and she had prominent blue eyes behind invisible pince-nez. Her face was long, like a sheep's, but she gave no impression of foolishness, rather of extreme alertness; she had the quick movements of a bird. The most remarkable thing about her was her voice, high, metallic, and without inflexion; it fell on the ear with a hard monotony, irritating to the nerves like the pitiless clamour of the pneumatic drill.

18. Read the following passage carefully and answer the questions concerning it.

She glanced at his face; it seemed much more dusky, and duskily ruddy, than she had known him. He was a stranger: and yet it was he, no other. He said nothing at all. But that was also in keeping. His mouth was closed, his watchful eyes seemed changeless, and there was a shadow of silence around him, impenetrable, but not cold. Rather aloof and gentle, like the silence that surrounds a wild animal.

She knew that she was walking with his spirit. But that even did not trouble her. It seemed natural. And there came over her again the feeling she had forgotten, the restful, thoughtless pleasure of a woman who moves in the aura of the man to whom she belongs. As a young woman she had had this unremarkable, yet very precious feeling, when she was with her husband. It had been a full contentment; and perhaps the fullness of it had made her unconscious of it. Later, it seemed to her she had almost wilfully destroyed it, this soft flow of contentment which she, a woman, had from him as a man.

Now, afterwards, she realized it. And as she walked at his side through the conquered city, she realized that it was the one enduring thing a woman can have, the intangible soft flood of contentment that carries her along at the side of the man she is married to. It is her perfection and her highest attainment.

Now, in the afterwards, she knew it. Now the strife was gone. And dimly she wondered why, why, why she had ever fought against it. No matter what the man does or is, as a person, if a woman can move at his side in this dim, full flood of contentment, she has the highest of him, and her scratching efforts at getting more than this are her ignominious efforts at self-nullity.

Now, she knew it, and she submitted. Now that she was walking with a man who came from the halls of death, to her, for her relief. The strong, silent kindliness of him towards her, even now, was able to wipe out the ashy, nervous horror of the world from her body. She went at his side, still and released, like one newly unbound, walking in the dimness of her own contentment.

At the bridge-head he came to a standstill, and drew his hand from her arm. She knew he was going to leave her. But he looked at her from under his peaked cap, darkly but kindly, and he waved his hand with a slight, kindly gesture of farewell, and of promise, as if in farewell he promised never to leave her, never to let the kindliness go out in his heart, to let it stay here always.

She hurried over the bridge with tears running down her cheeks, and on to her hotel. Hastily she climbed to her room. And as she

74

undressed, she avoided the sight of her own face in the mirror. She must not rupture the spell of his presence.

a. What attitude towards marriage do you find expressed in the passage?
b. By what means, and with what success, is the relationship between the man and the woman presented?

19. Read the following passage carefully, and answer the questions on it briefly, to the point, and in your own words.

In the days when the spinning-wheels hummed busily in the farm-houses — and even great ladies, clothed in silk and thread-lace, had their toy spinning-wheels of polished oak — there might be seen, in districts far away among the lanes, or deep in the bosom of the hills, certain pallid undersized men, who, by the side of the brawny countryfolk, looked like the remnants of a disinherited race. The shepherd's dog barked fiercely when one of these alien-looking men appeared on the upland, dark against the early winter sunset; for what dog likes a figure bent under a heavy bag? — and these pale men rarely stirred abroad without that mysterious burden. The shepherd himself, though he had good reason to believe that the bag held nothing but flaxen thread, or else the long rolls of strong linen spun from that thread, was not quite sure that this trade of weaving, indispensable though it was, could be carried on entirely without the help of the Evil One. In that far-off time superstition clung easily round every person or thing that was at all unwonted, or even intermittent and occasional merely, like the visits of the pedlar or the knife-grinder. No one knew where wandering men had their homes or their origin; and how was a man to be explained unless you at least knew somebody who knew his father and mother? To the peasants of old times, the world outside their own direct experience was a region of vagueness and mystery: to their untravelled thought a state of wandering was a conception as dim as the winter life of the swallows that came back with the spring; and even a settler, if he came from distant parts, hardly ever ceased to be viewed with a remnant of distrust, which would have prevented any surprise if a long course of inoffensive conduct on his part had ended in the commission of a crime; especially if he had any reputation for knowledge, or showed any skill in handicraft. All cleverness, whether in the rapid use of that difficult instrument the tongue, or in some other art unfamiliar to villagers, was in itself suspicious: honest folks, born and bred in a visible manner, were mostly not over-wise or clever — at least, not beyond such a matter as knowing the signs of the weather; and the process by which rapidity and dexterity of any kind were acquired was so wholly hidden, that they partook of the nature of conjuring. In this way it came to pass that those scattered linen-weavers — emigrants from the town into the country — were to the last regarded as aliens by their rustic neighbours, and usually contracted the eccentric habits which belong to a state of loneliness.

a. What meaning do you attach to the phrase 'the remnants of a disinherited race' (11. 6–7) as it appears in the context of this passage?

b. What justification does the author give for the statement 'All cleverness . . . was in itself suspicious' (11. 32–35)?

c. What do you think the author's attitude is towards village life?

20. Read the following passage carefully and answer the questions concerning it.

Late in October the first snow had come, large heavy flakes with shaggy edges, far apart, moving down in vast circles from a soft sky. The trees in the orchard outside the window of the dining-room were hard and cold, and shone like smooth rock against the earth and the colorless air. And the big rough flakes moved cautiously among them, here and there, as if exploring the terrain. There was a slight flurry, and the flakes gathered faster; then followed flurry upon flurry, a few moments apart, a steady slow pulsation, and with each the air was whiter and darker, till at last, the flurries coming imperceptibly closer and closer together, the air was an unbroken sheet of snow through which one could hardly move, the flakes were small and quick, and darkness, amid the confusion, had superseded twilight.

During the winter months the snow had laid deep over the rounded hills, and I had gone out on skis with my two Airedales. The clouds were of a soft even gray, and they seemed to have no lower edges, so that the sky had no identity — there was merely the soft air. The snow merged into the air from below with no visible dividing line. Often I should not have known whether I was going uphill or down, had it not been for the pull of gravity and the visible inclination of the skis. Often I came to the top of a rise and started down with no warning save the change in speed, or arrived at the bottom of a hill with no warning save the sudden slowing. I could travel for miles and see only one or two houses. Sometimes a mouse appeared, floundering as if in heavy air, and the dogs would lunge clumsily after it, snap it up, and drop it dead, leaving a small spot of blood suspended in grayness: but the few rabbits were better equipped and evaded them.

Once I passed a small pen made of chicken-wire, behind a barn, a pen in which there were fifteen or eighteen yearling coyotes. The farmers often captured the cubs during the spring plowing, and kept them into the next winter in order to slaughter them for the fur. These were about ready for killing. They swung in a group to the fence as I passed, lifting the foreparts of their bodies swiftly and gently, to drop them precisely facing, their shoulders flat, the front legs straight and close together, the wide sharp ears erect, the narrow little noses examining the air detail by detail. It was strange that they never broke through so slight a fence, yet there they were; young dogs would have torn through it with scarcely a pause, scarcely the sense of an obstacle. But these creatures were innocent and delicate, spirits impeded by a spell, puffs of smoke precise at the tips. As I passed, they turned their heads, watching me, then moved away and apart, to lie down in the snow or crawl under their small shelter. They had been the only sign of life amid four hours of snow, and they had made no sound. They had focused upon me for a moment their changing, shadowy curiosity, and then had been dissipated as if by the quiet of the hills.

a. Give a brief account of the events being described in this passage.
b. Write a critical appraisal of the passage, paying attention to the state of mind that is being presented and how the writer achieves his effects.

21. Write a critical appraisal of the prose passage printed below.

Presently at a place where the river flowed round a headland of the meadows, we stopped a while for rest and victuals, and settled ourselves on a beautiful bank which almost reached the dignity of a hillside: the wide meadows spread before us, and already the scythe was busy amidst the hay. One change I noticed amidst the quiet beauty of the fields — to wit, that they were planted with trees here and there, often fruit-trees, and that there was none of the niggardly begrudging of space to a handsome tree which I remembered too well, and though the willows were often polled (or shrowded, as they call it in that countryside), this was done with some regard to beauty: I mean that there was no polling of rows on rows so as to destroy the pleasantness of half a mile of country, but a thoughtful sequence in the cutting, that prevented a sudden bareness anywhere. To be short, the fields were everywhere treated as a garden made for the pleasure as well as the livelihood of all, as old Hammond told me was the case.

On this bank or bent of the hill, then, we had our mid-day meal; somewhat early for dinner, if that mattered, but we had been stirring early: the slender stream of the Thames winding below us between the garden of a country I have been telling of; a furlong from us was a beautiful little islet begrown with graceful trees; on the slopes westward of us was a wood of varied growth overhanging the narrow meadow on the south side of the river; while to the north was a wide stretch of mead rising very gradually from the river's edge. A delicate spire of an ancient building rose up from out of the trees in the middle distance, with a few grey houses clustered about it; while nearer to us, in fact not half a furlong from the water, was a quite modern stone house — a wide quadrangle of one storey, the buildings that made it being quite low. There was no garden between it and the river, nothing but a row of pear trees still quite young and slender; and though there did not seem to be much ornament about it, it had a sort of natural elegance, like that of the trees themselves.

As we sat looking down on all this in the sweet June day, rather happy than merry, Ellen, who sat next to me, her hand clasped about one knee, leaned sideways to me, and said in a low voice which Dick and Clara might have noted if they had not been busy in happy wordless love-making: "Friend, in your country were the houses of your field-labourers anything like that?"

22. The following passage is the beginning of a short story. Read it carefully and answer the questions on it:

There was a woman who was beautiful, who started with all the advantages, yet she had no luck. She married for love, and the love turned to dust. She had bonny children, yet she felt they had been thrust upon her, and she could not love them. They looked at her coldly, as if they were finding fault with her. And hurriedly she felt she must cover up some fault in herself. Yet what it was that she must cover up she never knew. Nevertheless, when her children were present, she always felt the centre of her heart go hard. This troubled her, and in her manner she was all the more gentle and anxious for her children, as if she loved them very much. Only she herself knew that at the centre of her heart was a hard little place that could not feel love, no, not for anybody. Everybody else said of her: 'She is such a good mother. She adores her children.' Only she herself, and her children themselves, knew it was not so. They read it in each other's eyes.

There was a boy and two little girls. They lived in a pleasant house, with a garden, and they had discreet servants, and felt themselves superior to anyone in the neighbourhood.

Although they lived in style, they felt always an anxiety in the house. There was never enough money. The mother had a small income, and the father had a small income, but not nearly enough for the social position which they had to keep up. The father went into town to some office. But though he had good prospects, these prospects never materialized. There was always the grinding sense of the shortage of money, though the style was always kept up.

At last the mother said: 'I will see if *I* can't make something.' But she did not know where to begin. She racked her brains, and tried this thing and the other, but could not find anything successful. The failure made deep lines come into her face. Her children were growing up, they would have to go to school. There must be more money, there must be more money. The father, who was always very handsome and expensive in his tastes, seemed as if he never *would* be able to do anything worth doing. And the mother, who had a great belief in herself, did not succeed any better, and her tastes were just as expensive.

And so the house came to be haunted by the unspoken phrase: *There must be more money! There must be more money!* The children could hear it all the time, though nobody said it aloud. They heard it at Christmas, when the expensive and splendid toys filled the nursery. Behind the shining modern rocking-horse, behind the smart doll's house, a voice would start whispering: 'There *must* be more money! There *must* be more money!' And the children would stop playing, to listen for a moment. They would look into each other's eyes, to see if they had all heard. And each one saw in the eyes of the other two that they too had heard. 'There *must* be more money! There *must* be more money!

It came whispering from the springs of the still-swaying rocking-horse, and even the horse, bending his wooden, champing head, heard it. The big doll, sitting so pink and smirking in her new pram, could hear it quite plainly, and seemed to be smirking all the more self-consciously because of it. The foolish puppy, too, that took the place of the teddy-bear, he was looking so extraordinarily foolish for no other reason but that he heard the secret whisper all over the house. 'There *must* be more money!'

Yet nobody ever said it aloud. The whisper was everywhere, and therefore no one spoke it. Just as no one ever says: 'We are breathing!' in spite of the fact that breath is coming and going all the time.

a. What sense of the importance of money does the author convey here? Does he approve of the way the family 'lived in style', or not?

b. Do you think the author has succeeded in creating an interest in his characters, and in what is going to happen next? Support your view with reasons.

23. Compare and contrast the treatment, in the following two passages, of

a place to live in. Try to support your answer by specific examples drawn from the passage, paying attention at the same time to the quality of the writing, especially to the rhythm and choice of words.

(a) All, as they approached, looked upward at the imposing edifice, which was henceforth to assume its rank among the habitations of mankind. There it rose, a little withdrawn from the life of the street, but in pride, not modesty. Its whole visible exterior was ornamented with quaint figures, conceived in the grotesqueness of a gothic fancy, and drawn or stamped in the glittering plaster, composed of lime, pebbles, and bits of glass, with which the wood-work of the walls was overspread. On every side, the seven gables pointed sharply towards the sky, and presented the aspect of a whole sisterhood of edifices, breathing through the spiracles of one great chimney. The many lattices, with their small, diamond-shaped panes, admitted the sunlight into hall and chamber, while, nevertheless, the second story, projecting far over the base, and itself retiring beneath the third, threw a shadowy and thoughtful gloom into the lower rooms. Carved globes of wood were affixed under the jutting stories. Little spiral rods of iron beautified each of the seven peaks. On the triangular portion of the gable that fronted next the street, was a dial, put up that very morning, and on which the sun was still marking the passage of the first bring hour in a history that was not destined to be all so bright. All around were scattered shavings, chips, shingles, and broken halves of bricks; these, together with the lately turned earth, on which the grass had not begun to grow, contributed to the impression of strangeness and novelty proper to a house that had yet its place to make among men's daily interests.

The principal entrance, which had almost the breadth of a church-door, was in the angle between the two front gables, and was covered by an open porch, with benches beneath its shelter. Under this arched door-way, scraping their feet on the unworn threshold, now trod the clergymen, the elders, the magistrates, the deacons, and whatever of aristocracy there was in town or county. Thither, too, thronged the plebeian classes, as freely as their betters, and in larger number. Just within the entrance, however, stood two serving-men, pointing some of the guests to the neighbourhood of the kitchen, and ushering others into the statelier rooms, — hospitable alike to all, but still with a scrutinising regard to the high or low degree of each. Velvet garments, sombre but rich, stiffly-plaited ruffs and bands, embroidered gloves, venerable beards, the mien and countenance of authority, made it easy to distinguish the gentleman of worship, at the period, from the tradesman, with his plodding air, or the labourer, in his leathern jerkin, stealing awe-stricken into the house which he had perhaps helped to build.

(b) But let me have a night in late November, let us say. Every leaf has long been down, save that the beech hedgerow in the sheltered forest road will keep its tawny copper all through the winter. Rain has been sweeping along the valleys for days past in giant misty pillars, the brooks are bank high with red, foaming water; down every steep field little hedgerow streams come pouring. In the farmyards the men go about their work clad in sacks, and if they may well shelter under penthouses and find work to do in the barns.

Give me a night in the midst of such weather, and then think of the farm atop the hill, to which two good miles of deep, wandering lane go climbing, and mix the rain with a great wind from the mountain: and then think of entering the place which I have described, set now for the old act of winter. The green shutters are close fastened without the window, the settle is curved about the hearth, and that great cavern is ablaze and glorious with heaped wood and coals, and the white walls golden with the light of the leaping flames. And those within can hear the rain dashing upon shutter and upon closed door, and the fire hisses now and again as stray drops fall down the chimney; and the great wind shakes the trees and goes roaring down the hillside to the valley and moans and mutters about the housetop.

A man will leave his place, snug in shelter, in the deepest glow of the fire, and go out for a moment and open but a little of the door in the porch and see all the world black and wild and wet, and then come back to the light and heat and thank God for his home, wondering whether any are still abroad on such a night of tempest.

24. Read the following passage carefully and answer the questions on it briefly and to the point.

Every man's nature is a sufficient advertisement to him of the character of his fellow. My right and my wrong is their right and their wrong. Whilst I do what is fit for me, and abstain from what is unfit, my neighbour and I shall often agree in our means, and work together for a time to one end. But whenever I find my dominion over myself not sufficient for me, and undertake the direction of him also, I overstep the truth, and come into false relations to him. I may have so much more skill or strength than he, that he cannot express adequately his sense of wrong, but it is a lie, and hurts like a lie both him and me. Love and nature cannot maintain the assumption: it must be

81

executed by a practical lie, namely, by force. This undertaking for another, is the blunder which stands in colossal ugliness in the governments of the world. It is the same thing in numbers, as in a pair, only
not quite so intelligible. I can see well enough a great difference
between my setting myself down to a self-control, and my going to
make somebody else act after my views: but when a quarter of the
human race assume to tell me what I must do, I may be too much disturbed by the circumstances to see so clearly the absurdity of their
command. Therefore, all public ends look vague and quixotic beside
private ones. For, any laws but those which men make for themselves,
are laughable. If I put myself in the place of my child, and we stand in
one thought, and see that things are thus or thus, that perception is
law for him and me. We are both there, both act. But if, without
carrying him into the thought, I look over into his plot, and, guessing
how it is with him, ordain this or that, he will never obey me. This is
the history of governments — one man does something which is to
bind another. A man who cannot be acquainted with me taxes me
looking from afar at me, ordains that a part of my labour shall go to
this or that whimsical end, not as I, but as he happens to fancy.
Behold the consequence. Of all debts, men are least willing to pay the
taxes. What a satire is this on government! Everywhere they think
they get their money's worth, except for these.

Hence, the less government we have, the better — the fewer laws,
and the less confided power. The antidote to this abuse of formal
government is, the influence of private character, the growth of the
Individual; the appearance of the principal to supersede the proxy; the
appearance of the wise man, of whom the existing government is, it
must be owned, but a shabby imitation. That which all things tend to
educe, which freedom, cultivation, intercourse, revolutions, go to
form and deliver, is character; that is the end of nature, to reach unto
this coronation of her king. To educate the wise man, the State exists;
and with the appearance of the wise man, the State expires. The
appearance of character makes the State unnecessary. The wise man is
the State. He needs no army, fort, or navy — he loves men too well;
no bride, or feast, or palace to draw friends to him; no vantage
ground, no favourable circumstance. He needs no library, for he has
not done thinking; no church, for he is a prophet; no statute book, for
he has the lawgiver; no money, for he is value; no road, for he is at
home where he is; no experience, for the life of the creator shoots
through him, and looks from his eyes. He has no personal friends, for
he who has the spell to draw the prayer and piety of all men unto him,
needs not husband and educate a few, to share with him a select and

poetic life. His relation to men is angelic; his memory is myrrh to them; his presence, frankincense and flowers.

a. Say what meaning you attach in the context of this passage to the statement: 'This undertaking for another, is the blunder which stands in colossal ugliness in the governments of the world' (lines 11–13).
b. What reasons are given in justification of the statement ' . . . all public ends look vague and quixotic* beside private ones' (lines 19–20)?
c. By reference to the passage explain what you understand by the following assertions: 'To educate the wise man, the State exists; and with the appearance of the wise man, the State expires. The appearance of character makes the State unnecessary. The wise man is the State' (lines 41–44).
d. By what means, and how convincingly, does the author advance his argument?

* idealistic and utterly impractical

25. The following two passages have in common the description of buildings, one a cathedral and the other an ancient and ruined castle. Read them both carefully and answer the questions concerning them.

(a) What else there is of light is from torches, or silver lamps burning ceaselessly in the recesses of the chapels; the roof sheeted with gold, and the polished walls covered with alabaster, give back at every curve and angle some feeble gleaming to the flames; and the glories round the heads of the sculptured saints flash out upon us as we pass them, and sink again into the gloom. Under foot and over head, a continual succession of crowded imagery, one picture passing into another, as in a dream; forms beautiful and terrible mixed together; dragons and serpents, and ravening beasts of prey, and graceful birds that in the midst of them drink from running fountains and feed from vases of crystal; the passions and the pleasures of human life symbolized together, and the mystery of its redemption; for the mazes of interwoven lines and changeful pictures lead always at last to the Cross, lifted and carved in every place and upon every stone; sometimes with the serpent of eternity wrapt round it, sometimes with doves beneath its arms, and sweet herbage growing forth from its feet; but conspicuous most of all on the great rood that crosses the church before the altar, raised in bright blazonry against the shadow of the apse.

Through the heavy door whose bronze network closes the place of his rest, let us enter the church itself. It is lost in still deeper twilight, to which the eye must be accustomed for some moments before the form of the building can be traced; and then there opens before us a vast cave, hewn out into the form of a Cross, and divided into shadowy aisles by many pillars. Round the domes of its roof the light enters only through narrow apertures like large stars; and here and there a ray or two from some far-away casement wanders into the darkness, and casts a narrow phosphoric stream upon the waves of marble that heave and fall in a thousand colours along the floor.

(b) The roar of the storm can be heard travelling the complete circuit of the castle — a measured mile — coming around at intervals like a circumambulating column of infantry. Doubtless such a column has passed this way in its time, but the only columns which enter in these latter days are the columns of sheep and oxen that are sometimes seen here now; while the only semblance of heroic voices heard are the utterances of such, and of the many winds which make their passage through the ravines.

The expected lightning radiates round, and a rumbling as from its subterranean vaults — if there are any — fills the castle. The lightning repeats itself, and, coming after the aforesaid thoughts of martial men, it bears a fanciful resemblance to swords moving in combat. It has the very brassy hue of the ancient weapons that here were used. The so sudden entry upon the scene of this metallic flame is as the entry of a presiding exhibitor who unrolls the maps, uncurtains the pictures, unlocks the cabinets, effects a transformation by merely exposing the material of his science, unintelligibly cloaked till then. The abrupt configuration of the bluffs and mounds now for the first time clearly revealed — mounds whereon, doubtless, spears and shields have frequently lain while their owners loosened their sandals and yawned and stretched their arms in the sun. For the first time, too, a glimpse is obtainable of the true entrance used by its occupants of old, some way ahead.

There, where all passage has seemed to be inviolably barred by an almost vertical facade, the ramparts are found to overlap each other like loosely clasped fingers, between which a zigzag path may be followed — a cunning construction that puzzles the uninformed eye. But its cunning, even where not obscured by dilapidation, is now wasted on the solitary forms of a few wild badgers, rabbits, and hares. Men must have often gone out by those gates in the morning to battle with the Roman legions under Vespasian; some to return no more, others to come back at evening, bringing with them the noise of their heroic deeds. But not a page, not a stone, has preserved their fame.

a. Compare and contrast the use of imagery in the two passages.

b. Consider the part played by rhythm and syntax in creating the effect of each passage.

c. Consider the tone of each passage, saying what you take in each case to be the central concern.

26. The passage given below is a description of an island in the South Pacific, near the Equator and off the coast of Peru. It is called Rodondo. Read the passage carefully and answer the questions on it.

My first visit to the spot was made in the gray of the morning. With a view of fishing, we had lowered three boats, and pulling some two miles from our vessel, found ourselves just before dawn of day close under the moon-shadow of Rodondo. Its aspect was heightened, and yet softened, by the strange double twilight of the hour. The great full moon burnt in the low west like a half-spent beacon, casting a soft mellow tinge upon the sea like that cast by a waning fire of embers upon a midnight hearth; while along the entire east the invisible sun sent pallid intimations of his coming. The wind was light; the waves languid; the stars twinkled with a faint effulgence; all nature seemed supine with the long night watch, and half-suspended in jaded expectation of the sun. This was a critical hour to catch Rodondo in his perfect mood. The twilight was just enough to reveal every striking point, without tearing away the dim investiture of wonder.

From a broken stair-like base, washed, as the steps of a water-palace, by the waves, the tower rose in entablatures of strata to a shaven summit. Those uniform layers, which compose the mass, form its most peculiar feature. For at their lines of junction they project flatly into encircling shelves, from top to bottom, rising one above another in graduated series. And as the eaves of any old barn or abbey are alive with swallows, so were all these rocky ledges with unnumbered sea-fowl. Eaves upon eaves, and nests upon nests. Here and there were long birdlime streaks of a ghostly white staining the tower from sea to air, readily accounting for its sail-like look afar. All would have been bewitchingly quiescent, were it not for the demoniac din created by the birds. Not only were the eaves rustling with them, but they flew densely overhead, spreading themselves into a winged and continually shifting canopy. The tower is the resort of aquatic birds for hundreds of leagues around. To the north, to the east, to the west, stretches nothing but eternal ocean; so that the man-of-war hawk coming from the coasts of North America, Polynesia, or Peru, makes his first land at Rodondo. And yet though Rodondo be terra-firma, no landbird ever lighted on it. Fancy a red-robin or a canary there! What a falling into the hands of the Philistines, when the poor warbler should be surrounded by such locust-flights of strong bandit birds with long bills cruel as daggers.

a. State briefly what impressions of the island the passage gives you.
b. How clearly are these impressions presented?

27. Compare and contrast the treatment, in the following two passages, of the natural world. You should pay attention to the language used, especially to rhythm and phrasing.

(a) I have spoken of the two openings into the vale. From the one to the north-west issued a rivulet, which came, gently murmuring and slightly foaming, down the ravine, until it dashed against the group of rocks out of which sprang the insulated hickory. Here, after encircling the tree, it passed on a little to the north of east, leaving the tulip tree some twenty feet to the south, and making no decided alteration in its course until it came near the midway between the eastern and western boundaries of the valley. At this point, after a series of sweeps, it turned off at right angles and pursued a generally southern direction — meandering as it went — until it became lost in a small lake of irregular figure (although roughly oval), that lay gleaming near the lower extremity of the vale. This lakelet was, perhaps, a hundred yards in diameter at its widest part. No crystal could be clearer than its waters. Its bottom, which could be distinctly seen, consisted altogether of pebbles brilliantly white. Its banks, of the emerald grass already described, *rounded*, rather than sloped, off into the clear heaven below; and so clear was this heaven, so perfectly, at times, did it reflect all objects above it, that where the true bank ended and where the mimic one commenced, it was a point of no little difficulty to determine. The trout, and some other varieties of fish, with which this pond seemed to be almost inconveniently crowded, had all the appearance of veritable flying fish. It was almost impossible to believe that they were not absolutely suspended in the air. A light birch canoe that lay placidly on the water was reflected in its minutest fibres with a fidelity unsurpassed by the most exquisitely polished mirror. A small island, fairly laughing with flowers in full bloom, and affording little more space than just enough for a picturesque little building, seemingly a fowl-house — arose from the lake not far from its northern shore to which it was connected by means of an inconceivably light-looking and yet very primitive bridge. It was formed of a single, broad and thick plank of the tulip wood. This was forty feet long, and spanned the interval between shore and shore with a slight but very perceptible arch, preventing all oscillation. From the southern extreme of the lake issued a continuation of the rivulet, which, after meandering for, perhaps, thirty yards, finally passed through the depression (already described) in the middle of the southern declivity, and tumbling down a sheer precipice of a hundred feet, made its devious and unnoticed way to the Hudson.

(b) But in the morning it is quite different. Then the sun shines strong on the horizontal green cloud-puffs of the pines, the sky is clear and full of life, the water runs hastily, still browned by the last juice of crushed olives. And there the earth's bowl of crocuses is amazing. You cannot believe that the flowers are really still. They are open with such delight and their pistil-thrust is so red-orange, and they are so many, all reaching out wide and marvellous, that it suggests a perfect ecstasy of radiant, thronging movement, lit-up violet and orange, and surging in some invisible rhythm of concerted, delightful movement. You cannot believe they do not move, and make some sort of crystalline sound of delight. If you sit still and watch, you begin to move with them, like moving with the stars, and you feel the sound of their radiance. All the little cells of the flowers must be leaping with flowery life and utterance.

And the small brown honey bees hop from flower to flower, dive down, try, and off again. The flowers have been already rifled, most of them. Only sometimes a bee stands on his head, kicking slowly inside the flower, for some time. He has found something. And all the bees have little loaves of pollen, bee-bread, in their elbow joints.

The crocuses last in their beauty for a week or so, and as they begin to lower their tents and abandon camp, the violets begin to thicken. It is already March. The violets have been showing like tiny dark hounds for some weeks. But now the whole pack comes forth, among the grass and the tangle of wild thyme, till the air all sways subtly scented with violets, and the banks above where the crocuses had their tents are now swarming brilliant purple with violets. They are the sweet violets of early spring, but numbers have made them bold, for they flaunt and ruffle till the slopes are a bright blue purple blaze of them, full in the sun, with an odd late crocus still standing wondering and erect amongst them.

And now that it is March, there is a rush of flowers. Down by the other stream, which turns sideways to the sun, and has tangles of brier and bramble, down where the hellebore has stood so wan and dignified all winter, there are now white tufts of primroses, suddenly come. Among the tangle and near the water-lip, tufts and bunches of primroses, in abundance. Yet they look more wan, more pallid, more flimsy than English primroses. They lack some of the full wonder of the northern flowers. One tends to overlook them, to turn to the great, solemn-faced purple violets that rear up from the bank, and above all, to the wonderful little towers of the grape hyacinth.

28. Write a critical comparison of the following two passages, paying special attention to the treatment of the theme of the house.

(a) Evidently that gate is never opened: for the long grass and the great hemlocks grow against it; and if it were opened, it is so rusty, that the force necessary to turn it on its hinges would be likely to pull down the square stone-built pillars, to the detriment of the two stone lionesses which grin with a doubtful carnivorous affability above a coat of arms, surmounting each of the pillars. It would be easy enough by the aid of the nicks in the stone pillars, to climb over the brick wall with its smooth stone coping; but by putting our eyes close to the rusty bars of the gate, we can see the house well enough, and all but the very corners of the grassy enclosure.

It is a very fine old place, of red brick, softened by a pale powdery lichen, which has dispersed itself with happy irregularity, so as to bring the red brick into terms of friendly companionship with the limestone ornaments surrounding the three gables, the windows, and the door-place. But the windows are patched with wooden panes, and the door, I think, is like the gate — it is never opened: how it would groan and grate against the stone floor if it were! For it is a solid, heavy, handsome door, and must once have been in the habit of shutting with a sonorous bang behind a liveried lackey, who had just seen his master and mistress off the grounds in a carriage and pair.

But at present one might fancy the house in the early stage of a chancery suit, and that the fruit from that grand double row of walnut-trees on the right hand of the enclosure would fall and rot among the grass, if it were not that we heard the booming bark of dogs echoing from great buildings at the back. And now the half-weaned calves that have been sheltering themselves in a gorse-built hovel against the left-hand wall, come out and set up a silly answer to that terrible bark, doubtless supposing that it has reference to buckets of milk.

(b) The old-fashioned, low wainscoting went round the rooms, and up the staircase with carved balusters and shadowy angles, landing half-way up at a broad window, with a swallow's nest below the sill, and the blossom of an old pear-tree showing across it in late April, against the blue, below which the perfumed juice of the find of fallen

88

fruit in autumn was so fresh. At the next turning came the closet which held on its deep shelves the best china. Little angel faces and reedy flutings stood out round the fireplace of the children's room. And on the top of the house, above the large attic, where the white mice ran in the twilight — an infinite, unexplored wonderland of childish treasures, glass beads, empty scent-bottles still sweet, thrum[1] of coloured silks, among its lumber — a flat space of roof, railed round, gave a view of the neighbouring steeples; for the house, as I said, stood near a great city, which sent up heavenwards, over the twisting weather-vanes, not seldom, its beds of rolling cloud and smoke, touched with storm or sunshine. But the child of whom I am writing did not hate the fog, because of the crimson lights which fell from it sometimes upon the chimneys and the whites which gleamed through its openings, on summer mornings, on turret or pavement. For it is false to suppose that a child's sense of beauty is dependent on any choiceness or special fineness, in the objects which present themselves to it, though this indeed comes to be the rule with most of us in later life; earlier, in some degree, we see inwardly; and the child finds for itself, and with unstinted delight, a difference for the sense, in those whites and reds through the smoke on very homely buildings, and in the gold of the dandelions at the road-side, just beyond the houses, where not a handful of earth is virgin and untouched, in the lack of better ministries to its desire of beauty.

[1] *thrum* = threads remaining on loom when woven fabric has been cut off

29. Read the following passage carefully and answer the questions concerning it.

He was working on the edge of the common, beyond the small brook that ran in the dip at the bottom of the garden, carrying the garden path in continuation from the plank bridge on to the common. He had cut the rough turf and bracken, leaving the grey, dryish soil bare. But he was worried because he could not get the path straight, there was a pleat between his brows. He had set up his sticks, and taken the sights between the big pine trees, but for some reason everything seemed wrong. He looked again, straining his keen blue eyes, that had a touch of the Viking in them, through the shadowy pine trees as through a doorway, at the green-grassed garden-path rising from the shadow of alders by the log bridge up to the sunlit flowers. Tall white and purple columbines, and the butt-end of the old Hampshire cottage that crouched near the earth amid flowers, blossoming in the bit of shaggy wildness round about.

There was a sound of children's voices calling and talking: high, childish, girlish voices, slightly didactic and tinged with domineering: 'If you don't come quick, nurse, I shall run out there to where there are snakes.' And nobody had the *sangfroid* to reply: 'Run then, little fool.' It was always, 'No, darling. Very well, darling. In a moment, darling. Darling, you *must* be patient.'

His heart was hard with disillusion: a continual gnawing and resistance. But he worked on. What was there to do but submit!

The sunlight blazed down upon the earth, there was a vividness of flamy vegetation, of fierce seclusion amid the savage peace of the commons. Strange how the savage England lingers in patches: as here, amid these shaggy gorse commons, and marshy, snake infested places near the foot of the south downs. The spirit of place lingering on primeval, as when the Saxons came, so long ago.

Ah, how he had loved it! The green garden path, the tufts of flowers, purple and white columbines, and great oriental red poppies with their black chaps and mulleins tall and yellow, this flamy garden which had been a garden for a thousand years, scooped out in the little hollow among the snake-infested commons. He had made it flame with flowers, in a sun cup under its hedges and trees. So old, so old a place! And yet he had re-created it.

The timbered cottage with its sloping, cloak-like roof was old and forgotten. It belonged to the old England of hamlets and yeomen. Lost all alone on the edge of the common, at the end of a wide, grassy, briar-entangled lane shaded with oak, it had never known the world of today. Not till Egbert came with his bride. And he had come to fill it with flowers.

The house was ancient and very uncomfortable. But he did not want to alter it. Ah, marvellous to sit there in the wide, black, time-old chimney, at night when the wind roared overhead, and the wood which he had chopped himself sputtered on the hearth! Himself on one side the angle, and Winifred on the other.

Ah, how he had wanted her: Winifred! She was young and beautiful and strong with life, like a flame in sunshine. She moved with a slow grace of energy like a blossoming, red-flowered bush in motion. She, too, seemed to come out of the old England, ruddy, strong, with a certain crude, passionate quiescence and a hawthorn robustness. And he, he was tall and slim and agile, like an English archer with his long supple legs and fine movements. Her hair was nut-brown and all in energetic curls and tendrils. Her eyes were nut-brown, too, like a robin's for brightness. And he was white-skinned with fine, silky hair that had darkened from fair, and a slightly arched nose of an old country family. They were a beautiful couple.

a. Give a brief account of the relation between man and nature being presented here.
b. Say what your reaction to the passage is, making specific reference to the text.

30. Write a critical comparison of the texts printed below. You should pay close attention to the language used pointing to both differences and similarities in attitude and meaning.

(a) There are no natural objects out of which more can be learned than out of stones. They seem to have been created especially to reward a patient observer. Nearly all other objects in nature can be seen to some extent without patience and are pleasant even in being half seen. Trees, clouds, and rivers are enjoyable even by the careless; but the stone under his foot has, for carelessness, nothing in it but stumbling; no pleasure is languidly to be had out of it; nor food, nor good of any kind; nothing but symbolism of the hard heart, and the unfatherly gift. And yet, do but give it some reverence and watchfulness, and there is bread of thought in it, more than in any other lowly feature of all the landscape. For a stone, when it is examined, will be found a mountain in miniature. The fineness of Nature's work is so great, that into a single block, a foot or two in diameter, she can compress as many changes of form and structure, on a small scale, as she needs for her mountains on a large one, and taking moss for forests, and grains of crystal for crags, the surface of a stone in by fair the plurality of instances is more interesting than the surface of an ordinary hill; more fantastic in form, and incomparably richer in colour.

(b) Let me say — why not? — that yellow is the color of love. The reader may ask what I know of love, but I confront him with the same question. Unbendingly singular, almost harshly narrow, love — as it spreads out to encompass more and more — loses its power. So that a man who speaks of love speaks of his own meager handful of experiences with it — or of what passes for it. Abstract love, that love which powers religion and philosophy, has less to recommend it than the simple word that occurs over and over again in popular songs. Which, however, offer no solution to the bewildered lover. To love is to go consistently into the dark, perhaps even whistling. All the songs, poems, and novels that the mind drags with it testify to the fact that others are there in the blackness as well: sighing, groaning, or as it may be, howling. Yet the recording of these testaments goes on. We will never be done with it.

The poet says:

> the stain of love
> is upon the world!
> Yellow, yellow, yellow

— so I can claim a "precedent" for my assertion. It may be, though, that in flailing about, the notion that yellow is love's color appealed to my sense of design. I think of the pale sun that occasionally shines above the massive hotel: I think of Amarillo[1]. I think of the color of the walls in that tavern where the men still sit, drinking red beer. The peeling paint of those walls, a kind of dull mustard yellow, is close to the color I envision. Nothing spectacularly brilliant will do. The color is somehow perversely pleasing in its apposition to that which it surrounds. The men are caught within love itself, and play a song that details one of its facets.

[1]*Amarillo* the Spanish word for yellow; a town in New Mexico.

31. Compare and contrast the following passages, paying attention to the character of the experiences expressed and to the atmosphere created. You should comment in detail on the writing, including the rhythm, the choice of words and turns of phrase.

(a) At a small distance from the house my predecessor had made a seat overshadowed by a hedge of hawthorn and honeysuckle. Here, when the weather was fine and our labour soon finished, we usually sat together to enjoy an extensive landscape, in the calm of the evening. Here, too, we drank tea, which now was become an occasional banquet; and as we had it but seldom, it diffused a new joy, the preparations for it being made with no small share of bustle and ceremony. On these occasions our two little ones always read for us, and they were regularly served after we had done. Sometimes, to give a variety to our amusements, the girls sung to the guitar; and while they thus formed a little concert, my wife and I would stroll down the sloping field, that was embellished with blue-bells and centaury,* talk of our children with rapture, and enjoy the breeze that wafted both health and harmony.

In this manner we began to find that every situation in life may bring its own peculiar pleasures: every morning waked us to a repetition of toil, but the evening repaid it with vacant hilarity.

* A plant

92

(b) The scullery maid, before the plates came out, was cooling her cheeks by the lily pond.

There had always been lilies there, self-sown from wind-dropped seed, floating red and white on the green plates of their leaves. Water, for hundreds of years, had silted down into the hollow, and lay there four or five feet deep over a black cushion of mud. Under the thick plate of green water, glazed in their self-centred world, fish swam — gold, splashed with white, streaked with black or silver. Silently they manoeuvred in their water world, poised in the blue patch made by the sky, or shot silently to the edge where the grass, trembling, made a fringe of nodding shadow. On the water-pavement spiders printed their delicate feet. A grain fell and spiralled down; a petal fell, filled and sank. At that the fleet of boat-shaped bodies paused; poised; equipped; mailed; then with a waver of undulation off they flashed.

It was in that deep centre, in that black heart, that the lady had drowned herself. Ten years since the pool had been dredged and a thigh bone recovered. Alas, it was a sheep's, not a lady's. And sheep have no ghosts, for sheep have no souls. But, the servants insisted, they must have a ghost; the ghost must be a lady's; who had drowned herself for love. So none of them would walk by the lily pool at night, only now when the sun shone and the gentry still sat at table.

SOME USEFUL TERMS

The previous book *Poetry Appreciation for A-Level* provided a full glossary of necessary technical terms for both poetry and prose appreciation. The following is a short supplement of terms that the student may find particularly useful with regard to prose appreciation.

Affective

This describes any use of language intended to arouse particular feelings or emotion in the reader. Thus we may talk of the 'affective' associations or connotations of a word or phrase.

Characterization

The process by which a writer indicates the nature of his or her 'characters'. 'Character' may be revealed by the writer showing the reader the thoughts, or feelings, or motives of the fictional persona, by the things that the 'character' says or does, or by the things others say about him or her.

Elevated

A passage, or part of a passage, where the language and style are more formal, or grand, or poetic than normal. The adjective 'heightened' may also be used. Other terms for such writing — with more pejorative connotations — are 'high-flown', 'flowery' and 'purple passage'.

Emotive

A use of language designed to arouse deep emotion in the reader. 'Emotive' language will seek to make a more powerful impact than 'affective'.

Expressive	A type of language designed to communicate the writer's own emotions, feelings, or response.
Informative	A type of writing intended to 'inform'.
Interior Monologue	A technique of writing that attempts to give a deep impression of a mind 'talking' to itself, working out its thoughts and responses 'as they occur'.
Irony	Crucial to all types of writing. Basically it means stating one thing, yet implying — through tone or circumstance — something different (frequently the opposite). Irony is an effectively subtle means of 'indirectly' making an apt, or telling statement. It is likely to be lost if we 'miss' the writer's tone; this can result in serious 'mis-reading' of a passage.
Plot	The way in which a writer arranges a story or sequence of events. This is done to arrange the details of 'cause and effect' in the most significant order. E M Forster suggests a neat distinction between 'plot' and 'story'. "'The king died and then the queen died', is a story. 'The king died, and then the queen died of grief' is a plot".
Stream of Consciousness	A form of 'interior monologue' in which every aspect of the writing — rhythm, grammar, language, etc. — attempts to imitate or convey the actual impression of the 'thought process' in action.

ACKNOWLEDGEMENTS

For permission to quote from copyright material in this book we are grateful to the following copyright holders.

Reproduced by permission of The Bodley Head Ltd, for *Ulysses* by James Joyce; George Allen & Unwin Ltd, for *Education and The Social Order* by Bertrand Russell; J M Dent & Sons Ltd, for *Candide* by Voltaire; Jonathan Cape Ltd, for *Catch 22* by Joseph Heller; Laurence Pollinger Ltd & The Estate of Mrs Frieda Lawrence Ravagli, for two extracts from *Selected Essays* by D H Lawrence; Martin Secker & Warburg Ltd, for an extract from *The Holy Sinner* by Thomas Mann, translated by H T Lowe-Porter; Trustees of Joseph Conrad Estate, for *Lord Jim* by Joseph Conrad; University of Cambridge Local Examinations Syndicate for past years' examination papers and William Heinemann Ltd & The Bodley Head Ltd, for *The Comedians* by Graham Greene.

Let Sleeping Sea-Monsters Lie...

Eva Ibbotson was born in Vienna, but when the Nazis came to power her family fled to England and she was sent to boarding school. She became a writer while bringing up her four children, and her bestselling novels have been published around the world. Her books have also won and been shortlisted for many prizes. *Journey to the River Sea* won the Nestlé Gold Award and was runner-up for the Whitbread Children's Book of the Year and the Guardian Children's Fiction Prize. *The Star of Kazan* won the Nestlé Silver Award and was shortlisted for the Carnegie Medal. *The Secret of Platform 13* was shortlisted for the Smarties Prize, and *Which Witch?* was runner-up for the Carnegie Medal. *The Ogre of Oglefort* was shortlisted for the Guardian Children's Fiction Prize and the Roald Dahl Funny Prize. Eva Ibbotson died peacefully in October 2010 at the age of eighty